WHAT HAPPENED IN HISTORY?

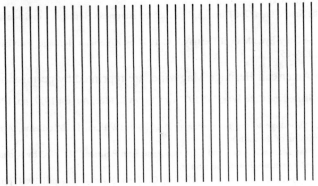

Edited by
Andrew Markham

Mt. San Antonio College

KENDALL/HUNT PUBLISHING COMPANY
2460 Kerper Boulevard P.O. Box 539 Dubuque, Iowa 52004-0539

The following articles are reprinted from *American Heritage* Magazine by special permission of American Heritage, a division of Forbes Inc.:

Bishop, Morris, "The Great Oneida Love-In," © 1969 by American Heritage, a division of Forbes Inc., February 1969, pp. 14–17, 86–92.

Foner, Eric, "The New View of Reconstruction," © 1983 by American Heritage, a division of Forbes Inc., October 1983, pp. 10–15.

Hofstadter, Richard, "America as a Gun Culture," © 1970 by American Heritage, a division of Forbes Inc., October 1970, pp. 4–11, 82–85.

Karp, Walter, "The Hour of the Founders," © 1974 by American Heritage, a division of Forbes Inc., June 1974, pp. 24–31.

Ketchum, Richard M., "Englands Vietnam," © 1971 by American Heritage a division of Forbes Inc., June 1971, pp. 6–11, 81–83.

O'Connor, Richard, "Mr. Coolidge's Jungle War," © 1967 by American Heritage, a division of Forbes Inc., December 1967, pp. 36–39, 89–93.

O'Connor, Richard, "Yanks in Siberia," © 1974 by American Heritage, a division of Forbes Inc., August 1974, pp. 10–17, 80–83.

Randel, William Pierce, "They Didn't Know What Time It Was," © 1983 by American Heritage, a division of Forbes Inc., October 1983, pp. 102–106.

Stewart, George R., "The Smart Ones Got Through," © 1955 by American Heritage, a division of Forbes Inc., June 1955, pp. 60–63, 108.

Wallace, Edward S., "The Gray-Eyed Man of Destiny," © 1957 by American Heritage, a division of Forbes Inc., December 1957, pp. 26–29, 123–25.

These articles from American Heritage Magazine, are reprinted by permission as noted:

Mee, Charles L., "Who Started the Cold War," © 1977 by Charles L. Mee, August 1977, pp. 10–15, reprinted by permission of the author.

Middleton, William D., "Goodbye to the Interurban," © 1966 by William D. Middleton, April 1966, pp. 30–41, 66–71, reprinted by permission of the author.

Wade, Richard C., "How the Media Seduced and Captured American Politics," © 1983 by Richard C. Wade, February 1983, pp. 46–53, reprinted by permission of the author.

Woodward, C. Vann, "The Birth of Jim Crow," © 1964 by C. Vann Woodward, April 1964, pp. 52–55, 100–3, reprinted by permission of the author.

Contents

Is A Textbook Enough?

An American History textbook provides the student with a quick overview, establishing a sense of continuity from the earliest times to the present. It also serves as a reference for specifics, being well stocked with dates and other details. A text is thus a necessary and valuable resource for students in a survey course.

However, textbooks are designed to be comprehensive, and this inevitably leads to a degree of superficiality. There is simply not enough space to go below the surface. Secondly, because they are designed to appeal to as wide an audience as possible, texts tend to avoid new or "controversial" interpretations for fear of alienating anyone. This all too often results in a book that is not only rather dry and bland, but one which may also reflect a naive and smug chauvinism. Much that is fascinating, thought-provoking, or amusing is left out. Not only are students given a distorted picture of their country's history, they can be misled as to what historians are really trying to do.

Historians, for the most part, are engaged in interpretation rather than mere description. They are trying to "make sense" of the past, rather than just pile up details. This book of readings can help the student develop a greater feel for history, and to "make sense" of the past. Hopefully this will generate an awareness that history is not just a description of things a lot of dead people did years ago; things that happened to *other* people before our time. Perhaps the student will come to realize that history is more realistically thought of as an analysis of a process we are all involved in; an exploration of the games we have all been playing. Without some such grasp of the reality of historical development, neither individuals nor nations are likely to thrive. Being unaware of the foundations on which we try to build is a dangerous business.

In this colleciton of articles we are reminded that an awareness of history helps us understand news stories as well as keep the media itself in perspective (Wade). It exposes the roots of serious problems in modern society (Hofstadter). It illuminates our relations with other countries, such as the Soviet Union (O'Connor, Yanks), (Mee and Harriman) or Nicaragua (Wallace), (O'Connor, Coolidge). Historical comparisons simultaneously enlighten us about the 18th Century and our recent past (Ketchum). History can give us a better understanding of *when* we are (Randel).

History is, of course, about people: the forceably included Afro-Americans and how they were kept "in their place" (Woodward). How did your grandparents get around? (Middleton). What can we learn from those who moved West (Stewart) or those who dropped out? (Bishop). And what about those in positions of power? Was "Tricky Dick" Nixon a crook? (Karp).

In this book all of these questions can be explored. We shall also see that sometimes historians' answers change with time. Did earlier historians *really* explain what happened after The War Between The States? (Foner).

Andrew Markham
Mt. San Antonio College

England's Vietnam: The American Revolution

Richard M. Ketchum

If it is true that those who cannot remember the past are condemned to repeat it, America's last three Presidents might have profited by examining the ghostly footsteps of America's last king before pursuing their adventure in Vietnam. As the United States concludes a decade of war in Southeast Asia, it is worth recalling the time, two centuries ago, when Britain faced the same agonizing problems in America that we have met in Vietnam. History seldom repeats itself exactly, and it would be a mistake to try to equate the ideologies or the motivating factors involved; but enough disturbing parallels may be drawn between those two distant events to make one wonder if the Messrs. Kennedy, Johnson, and Nixon had their ears closed while the class was studying the American Revolution.

Britain, on the eve of that war, was the greatest empire since Rome. Never before had she known such wealth and power; never had the future seemed so bright, the prospects so glowing. All, that is, except the spreading sore of discontent in the American colonies that, after festering for a decade and more, finally erupted in violence at Lexington and Concord on April 19, 1775. When news of the subsequent battle for Bunker Hill reached England that summer, George III and his ministers concluded that there was no alternative to using force to put down the insurrection. In the King's mind, at least, there was no longer any hope of reconciliation—nor did the idea appeal to him. He was determined to teach the rebellious colonials a les-

1

son, and no doubts troubled him as to the righteousness of the course he had chosen. "I am not sorry that the line of conduct seems now chalked out," he had said even before fighting began; later he told his prime minister, Lord North, "I know I am doing my Duty and I can never wish to retract." And then, making acceptance of the war a matter of personal loyalty, "I wish nothing but good," he said, "therefore anyone who does not agree with me is a traitor and a scoundrel." Filled with high moral purpose and confidence, he was certain that "when once these rebels have felt a smart blow, they will submit. . . ."

In British political and military circles there was general agreement that the war would be quickly and easily won. "Shall we be told," asked one of the King's men in Commons, "that [the Americans] can resist the powerful efforts of this nation?" Major John Pitcairn, writing home from Boston in March, 1775, said, "I am satisfied that one active campaign, a smart action, and burning two or three of their towns, will set everything to rights." The man who would direct the British navy during seven years of war, the unprincipled, inefficient Earl of Sandwich, rose in the House of Lords to express his opinion of the provincial fighting man. "Suppose the Colonies do abound in men," the First Lord of the Admiralty asked, "what does that signify? They are raw, undisciplined, cowardly men. I wish instead of forty or fifty thousand of these *brave* fellows they would produce in the field at least two hundred thousand; the more the better, the easier would be the conquest; if they did not run away, they would starve themselves into compliance with out measures. . . ." And General James Murray, who had succeeded the great Wolfe in 1759 as commander in North America, called the native American "a very effeminate thing, very unfit for and very impatient of war." Between these estimates of the colonial militiaman and a belief that the might of Great Britain was invincible, there was a kind of arrogant optimism in official quarters when the conflict began. "As there is not common sense in protracting a war of this sort," wrote Lord George Germain, the secretary for the American colonies, in September, 1775, "I should be for exerting the utmost force of this Kingdom to finish the rebellion in one campaign."

Optimism bred more optimism, arrogance more arrogance. One armchair strategist in the House of Commons, William Innes, outlined for the other members an elaborate scheme he had devised for the conduct of the war. First, he would remove the British troops from Boston, since that place was poorly situated for defense. Then, while the people of the Massachusetts Bay Colony were treated like the madmen they were and shut up by the navy, the army would move to one of the southern colonies, fortify itself in an impregnable position, and let the provincials attack if they pleased. The British could sally forth from this and other defensive enclaves at will, and eventually "success against one-half of America will pave the way to the conquest of the whole. . . ." What was more, Innes went on, it was "more than probable you may find men to recruit your army in America." There was a good possibility, in other words, that the British regulars would be replaced after a while by Americans who were loyal to their king, so that the army fighting the rebels would be Americanized, so to speak, and the Irish and English lads sent home. General James Robertson also believed that success lay in this scheme of Americanizing the combat force: "I never had an idea of subduing the Americans," he said, "I meant to assist the good Americans to subdue the bad."

This notion was important not only form the standpoint of the fighting, but in terms of administering the colonies once they were beaten; loyalists would take over the reins of government when the British pulled out, and loyalist militiamen would preserve order in the pacified colonies. No one knew, of course, how many "good" Americans there were; some thought they might make up half or more of the population. Shortly after arriving in the colonies in 1775, General William Howe, for one, was convinced that "the insurgents are very few, in comparison with the whole of the people."

Before taking the final steps into full-scale war, however, the King and his ministers had to be certain about one vitally important matter: they had to be able to count on the support of the English people. On several occasions in 1775 they were able to read the public pulse (that part of it, at least, that mattered) by observing certain important votes in Parliament. The King's address to both Houses on October 26, in which he announced plans to suppress the uprising in America, was followed by weeks of angry debate; but when the votes were counted, the North ministry's majority was overwhelming. Each vote indicated the full tide of anger that influenced the independent members, the country gentlemen who agreed that the colonials must be put in their place and taught a lesson. A bit out of touch with the news, highly principled, and content in the belief that the King and the ministry must be right, none of them seem to have asked what would be best for the empire; they simply went along with the vindictive measures that were being set in motion. Eloquent voices—those of Edmund Burke, Charles James Fox, The Earl of Chatham, John Wilkes, among others—were raised in opposition to the policies of the Crown, but as Burke said, ". . . it was almost in vain to contend, for the country gentlemen and abandoned their duty, and placed an implicit confidence in the Minister."

The words of sanity and moderation went unheeded because the men who spoke them were out of power and out of public favor; and each time the votes were tallied, the strong, silent, unquestioning majority prevailed. No one in any position of power in the government proposed, after the Battle of Bunker Hill, to halt the fighting in order to settle the differences; no one seriously contemplated conversations that might have led to peace. Instead the government—like so many governments before and since—took what appeared to be the easy way out and settled for war.

George III was determined to maintain his empire, intact and undiminished, and his greatest fear was that the loss of the American colonies would set off a reaction like a line of dominoes falling. Writing to Lord North in 1779, he called the contest with America "the most serious in which any country was ever engaged. In contains such a train of consequences that they must be examined to feel its real weight. . . . Independence is [the Americans'] object, which every man not willing to sacrifice every object to a momentary and inglorious peace must concur with me in thinking this country can never submit to. Should America succeed in that, the West Indies must follow, not in independence, but for their own interest they must become dependent on America. Ireland would soon follow, and this island reduced to itself, would be a poor island indeed."

Despite George's unalterable determination, strengthened by his domino theory; despite the wealth and might of the British empire; despite all the odds favoring a quick triumph, the problems facing the King and his ministers and the armed forces were formidable ones indeed. Surpassing all others in sheer magnitude was the immense distance between the mother country and the rebellious colonies. As Edmund Burke described the situation in his last, most eloquent appeal for conciliation, "Three thousand miles of ocean lie between you and them. No contrivance can prevent the effect of this distance in weakening government. Seas roll, and months pass, between the order and the execution; and the want of a speedy explanation of a single point is enough to defeat a whole system." Often the westerly passage took three months, and every soldier, every weapon, every button and gaiter and musket ball, every article of clothing and great quantities of food and even fuel, had to be shipped across those three thousand miles of the Atlantic. It was not only immensely costly and time consuming, but there was a terrifying wastefulness to it. Ships sank or were blown hundreds of miles off course, supplies spoiled, animals died en route, Worse yet, men died, and in substantial numbers: returns from regiments sent from the British Isles to the West Indies between 1776 and 1780 reveal that an average of 11 percent of the troops was lost on these crossings.

Beyond the water lay the North American land mass, and it was an article of faith on the part of many a British military man that certain ruin lay in fighting an enemy on any large scale in that savage wilderness. In the House of Lords in November, 1775, the Duke of Richmond warned the peers to consult their geographies before turning their backs on a peaceful settlement. There was, he said, "one insuperable difficulty with which an army would have to struggle"—America abounded in vast rivers that provided natural barriers to the progress of troops; it was a country in which every bush might conceal an enemy, a land whose cultivated parts would be laid waste, so that "the army (if any army could march or subsist) would be obliged to draw all its provisions from Europe, and all its fresh meat from Smithfield market." The French, the mortal enemies of Great Britain, who had seen a good deal more of the North American wild than the English had, were already laying plans to capitalize on the situation when the British army was bogged down there. In Paris, watchfully eyeing his adversary's every move, France's foreign minister, the Comte de Vergennes, predicted in July, 1775, that "it will be vain for the English to multiply their forces" in the colonies; "no longer can they bring that bast continent back to dependence by force of arms." Seven years later, as the war drew to a close, one of Rochambeau's aides told a friend of Charles James Fox: "No opinion was clearer than that though the people of America might be conquered by well disciplined European troops, the country of America was unconquerable."

Yet even in 1775 some thoughtful Englishmen doubted if the American people or their army could be defeated. Before the news of Bunker Hill arrived in London, the adjutant general declare that a plan to defeat the colonials militarily was "as wild an idea as ever controverted common sense," and the secretary-at-war, Lord Barrington, had similar reservations. As early as 1774 Barrington ventured the opinion that a war in the wilderness of North America would cost Britain far more than she could ever gain from it; that the size of the country and the colonials' familiarity with firearms would make victory questionable—or at best achievable only at the cost of enormous suffering; and finally, even if Britain should win such a contest, Barrington believed that the cost of maintaining the colonies in any state of subjection would be staggering. John Wilkes, taunting Lord North on this matter of military conquest, suggested that North—even if he rode out at the head of the entire English cavalry—would not venture ten miles into the countryside for fear of guerrilla fighters. "The Americans," Wilkes promised, "will dispute every inch of territory with you, every narrow pass, every strong defile, every Thermopylae, every Bunker's Hill."

It was left to the great William Pitt to provide the most stirring warning against fighting the Americans. Now Earl of Chatham, he was so crippled in mind and body that he rarely appeared in the House of Lords, but in May, 1777, he made the supreme effort, determined to raise his voice once again in behalf of conciliation. Supported on canes, his eyes flashing with the old fire and his beaklike face thrust forward belligerently, he warned the peers: "You cannot conquer the Americans. You talk of your numerous friends to annihilate the Congress, and of your powerful forces to disperse their army, but I might as well talk of driving them before me with this crutch. . . . You have been three years teaching them the art of war, and they are apt scholars. I will venture to tell your lordships that the American gentry will make officers enough fit to command the troops of all the European powers. What you have sent there are too many to make peace, too few to make war. You cannot make them respect you. You cannot make them wear your cloth. You will plant an invincible hatred in their breast against you . . ."

"My lords," he went on, "you have been the aggressors from the beginning. I say again, this country has been the aggressor. You have made descents upon their coasts. You have burnt their towns, plundered their country, made war upon the inhabitants, confiscated their property, proscribed and imprisoned their persons. . . . The people of America look upon Parliament as the authors of their miseries. Their affections are estranged from their sovereign. Let, then, reparation come from the hands that inflicted the injuries. Let conciliation succeed chastisement. . . ." But there was no persuading the majority; Chatham's appeal was rejected and the war went on unabated.

It began to appear, however, that destruction of the Continental Army—even if that goal could be achieved—might not be conclusive. After the disastrous campaign around Manhattan in 1776, George Washington had determined not to risk his army in a major engagement, and he began moving away from the European battle style in which two armies confronted each other head to head. His tactical method became that of the small, outweighed prizefighter who depends on his legs to keep him out of range of his opponent and who, when the bigger man begins to tire, darts in quickly to throw a quick punch, then retreats again. It was an approach to fighting described by Nathanael Greene, writing of the campaign in the South in 1780: "We fight, get beat, rise, and fight again." In fact, between January and September of the following year, Greene, short of money, troops, and supplies, won a major campaign without ever really winning a battle. The battle at Guilford Courthouse, which was won by the British, was typical of the results. As Horace Walpole observed, "Lord Cornwallis has conquered his troops out of shoes and provisions and himself out of troops."

There was, in the colonies, no great political center like Paris or London, whose loss might have been demoralizing to the Americans; indeed, Boston, New York, and Philadelphia, the seat of government, were all held at one time or another by the British without irreparable damage to the rebel cause. The fragmented political and military structure of the colonies was often a help to the rebels, rather than a hindrance, for it meant that there was almost no chance of the enemy striking a single crushing blow. The difficulty, as General Frederick Haldimand, who succeeded Carleton in Canada, saw it, was the seemingly unending availability of colonial militiamen who rose up out of nowhere to fight in support of the nucleus of regular troops called the Continental Army. "It is not the number of troops Mr. Washington can spare from his army that is to be apprehended," Haldimand wrote, "it is the multitude of militia and men in arms ready to turn out at an hour's notice at the shew of a single regiment of Continental Troops. . . ." So long as the British were able to split up their forces and fan out over the countryside in relatively small units, they were fairly successful in putting down the irregulars' activities and cutting off their supplies; but the moment they had to concentrate again to fight the Continentals, guerrilla warfare burst out like so many small brush fires on their flank and rear. No British regular could tell if an American was friend or foe, for loyalty to King George was easy to attest; and the man who was a farmer or merchant when a British battalion marched by his home was a militiaman as soon as it had passed by, ready to shoulder his musket when an emergency or an opportunity to confound the enemy arose.

Against an unnumberable supply of irregular forces the British could bring to bear only a fixed quantity of troops—however many, that is, they happened to have on the western side of the Atlantic Ocean at any given moment. Early in the war General James Murray had foreseen the difficulties that would undoubtedly arise. Writing to Lord Barrington, he warned that military conquest was no real answer. If the war proved to be a long one, their advantage in numbers would heavily favor the rebels, who could replace their losses while the British could not. Not only did every musket and grain of powder have to be shipped across the ocean; but if a man was killed or wounded, the only way to replace him was to send another man in full kit across the Atlantic. And troop transports were slow and small: three or four were required to move a single battalion.

During the summer of 1775 recruiting went badly in England and Ireland, for the war was not popular with a lot of the people who would have to fight it, and there were jobs to be had. It was evident that the only means of assembling a force large enough to suppress the rebellion in the one massive stroke that had been determined upon was to hire foreign troops. And immediately this word was out, the rapacious petty princes of Brunswick, Hesse-Cassel, and Waldeck, and the Margrave of Anspach-Bayreuth, generously offered up a number of their subjects—at a price—fully equipped and ready for duty, to serve His Majesty George III. Frederick the Great of Prussia, seeing the plan for what it was, announced that he would "make all the Hessian troops, marching through his dominions to

America, pay the usual cattle tax, because, although human beings, they had been sold as beasts.'' But George III and the princes regarded it as a business deal, in the manner of such dubious alliances ever since: each foot soldier and trooper supplied by the Duke of Brunswick, for instance, was to be worth seven pounds, four shillings, fourpence halfpenny in levy money to his Most Serene Highness. Three wounded men were to count as one killed in action, and it was stipulated that a soldier killed in combat would be paid for at the same rate as levy money. In other words the life of a subject was worth precisely seven pounds, four shillings, fourpence halfpenny to the Duke.

As it turned out, the large army that was assembled in 1776 to strike a quick, over-powering blow that would put a sudden end to the rebellion proved—when that decisive victory never came to pass—to be a distinct liability, a hideously expensive and at times vulnerable weapon. In the indecisive hands of men like William Howe and Henry Clinton, who never seemed absolutely certain about what they should do or how they should do it, the great army rarely had an opportunity to realize its potential; yet, it remained a ponderous and insatiable consumer of supplies, food, and money.

The loyalists, on whom many Englishmen had place such high hopes, proved a will-o'-the-wisp. Largely ignored by the policy makers early in the war despite their pleas for assistance, the loyalists were numerous enough but were neither well organized nor evenly distributed throughout the colonies. Where the optimists in Britain went wrong in thinking that loyalist strength would be an important factor was to imagine that anything like a majority of Americans *could* remain loyal to the Crown if they were not continuously sup-ported and sustained by the mother country. Especially as the war went on, as opinions har-dened, and as the possibility increased that the new government in America might actually survive, it was a very difficult matter to retain one's loyalty to the King unless friends and neighbors were of like mind and unless there was British force nearby to safeguard such a belief. Furthermore, it proved almost impossible for the British command to satisfy the loyalists, who were bitterly angry over the persecution and physical violence and robbery they had to endure and who charged constantly that the British generals were to lax in their treatment of rebels.

While the problems of fighting the war in distant American mounted, Britain found herself unhappily confronted with the combination of circumstances the Foreign Office dreaded most: with her armies tied down, the great European maritime powers—France and Spain—vengeful and adventurous and undistracted by war in the Old World, formed a coalition against her. When the American war began, the risk of foreign intervention was regarded as minimal, and the decision to fight was made on the premise that victory would be early and complete and that the armed forces would be released before any threatening European power could take advantage of the situation. But as the war continued without any definite signs of American collapse, France and Spain seized the chance to embarrass and perhaps humiliate their old antagonist. At first they supported the rebels surreptitiously with shipments of weapons and other supplied; then, when the situation appeared more auspicious, France in particular furnished active support in the form of an army and a navy, with catastrophic results for Great Britain.

One fascinating might-have-been is what would have happened had the Opposition in Parliament been more powerful politically. It consisted, after all, of some of the most forceful and eloquent orators imaginable, men whose words still have the power to send shivers up the spine. Not simply vocal, they were highly intelligent men whose concern went beyond the injustice and inhumanity of war. They were quick to see that the personal liberty of the King's subjects was as much an issue in London as it was in the colonies, and they foresaw irreparable damage to the empire if the government followed its unthinking policy of coercion. Given a stronger power base, they might have headed off war or the ultimate disaster; had the government been in the hands of men like Chatham or Burke or their followers, some accommodation with America might conceivable have evolved from the various proposals for reconciliation. But the King and North had the votes in their pockets, and the antiwar Opposition failed because a majority that was largely indifferent to reason supported the North ministry until the bitter end came with Cornwallis' surrender. Time and again a member of the Opposition would rise to speak out against the war for one reason or another: "This country," the Earl of Shelburne protested, "already burdened much beyond its abilities, is now on the eve of groaning under new taxes, for the purpose of carrying on this cruel and destructive war." Or, from Dr. Franklin's friend David Hartley: "Every proposition for reconciliation has so constantly and uniformly been crushed by Administration, that I think they seem not even to wish for the appearance of justice. The law of force is that which they appeal to. . . ." Or, from Sir James Lowther, when he learned that the King had rejected an "Olive Branch Petition" from the provincials: "Why have we not peace with a people who, it is evident, desire peace with us?" Or this, from General Henry Seymour Conway, inviting Lord North to inform members of the House of Commons about his overall program: "I do not desire the detail; let us have general outline, to be able to judge of the probability of its success. It is indecent not to lay before the House some plan, or the outlines of a plan. . . . If [the] plan is conciliation, let us see it, that we may form some opinion of it; if it be hostility and coercion, I do repeat, that we have no cause for a minute's consideration; for I can with confidence pronounce, that the present military armament will never succeed." But all unavailing, year after year, as each appeal to reason and humanity fell on ears deafened by self-righteousness and minds hardened against change.

Although it might be said that the arguments raised by the Opposition did not change the course of the war, they nevertheless affected the manner in which it was conducted, which in turn led to the ultimate British defeat. Whether Lord North was uncertain of that silent majority's loyalty is difficult to determine, but is seems clear that he was sufficiently nervous about public support to decide that a bold policy which risked defeats was not for him. As a result the war of the American Revolution was a limited war—limited from the standpoint of its objectives and the force with which Britain waged it.

In some respects the aspect of the struggle that may have had the greatest influence on the outcome was an intangible one. Until the outbreak of hostilities in 1775 no more than a small minority of the colonials had seriously contemplated independence, but after a year of war the situation was radically different. Now the mood was reflected in words such as these—instructions prepared by the county of Buckingham, in Virginia, for its delegates to a General Convention in Williamsburg: ". . . as far as your voices are admitted, you [will] cause a free and happy Constitution to be established, with a renunciation of the old, and so much thereof as has been found inconvenient and oppressive." That simple and powerful idea—renunciation of the old and its replacement with something new, independently conceived—was destined to sweep all obstacles before it. In Boston, James Warren was writing the news of home to John Adams in Philadelphia and told him: "Your Declaration of Independence came on Saturday and diffused a general joy. Every one of us feels more important than ever; we now congratulate each other as Freemen." Such winds of change were strong, and by contrast all Britain had to offer was a return to the status quo. Indeed, it was difficult for the average Englishman to comprehend the appeal that personal freedom and independence held for a growing number of Americans. As William Innes put it in a debate in Commons, all the government had to do to put an end to the nonsense in the colonies was to "convince the lower class of those infatuated people that the imaginary liberty they are so eagerly pursuing is not by any means to be compared to that which the Constitution of this happy country already permits them to enjoy."

With everything to gain from victory and everything to lose by defeat, the Americans could follow Livy's advice, that "in desperate matters the boldest counsels are the safest." Frequently beaten and disheartened, inadequately trained and fed and clothed, they fought on against unreasonably long odds because of that slim hope of attaining a distant goal. And as they fought on, increasing with each passing year the possibility that independence might be achieved, the people of Britain finally lost the will to keep going.

In England the goal had not been high enough, while the cost was too high. There was nothing compelling about the limited objective of bringing the colonies back into the empire, nothing inspiring about punishing the rebels, nothing noble in proving that retribution awaited those who would change the nature of things.

After the war had been lost and the treaty of peace signed, Lord North looked back on the whole affair and sadly informed the members of the House of Commons where, in his opinion, the fault lay. With a few minor changes, it was a message as appropriate to America in 1971 as to Britain in 1783: "The American war," he said, "has been suggested to have been the war of the Crown, contrary to the wishes of the people. I deny it. It was the war of Parliament. There was not a step taken in it that had not the sanction of Parliament. It was the war of the people, for it was undertaken for the express purpose of maintaining the just rights of Parliament, or, in other words, of the people of Great Britain, over the dependencies of the empire. For this reason, it was popular at its commencement, and eagerly embraced by the people and Parliament. . . . Nor did it ever cease to be popular until a series of unparalleled disasters and calamities caused the people, wearied out with almost uninterrupted ill-success and misfortune, to call out as loudly for peace as they had formerly done for war."

The Smart Ones Got Through

George R. Stewart

The difference between "an historical event" and "a dramatic event" is well illustrated by the stories of the Stevens Party and the Donner Party. The former is historically important, and the pioneers who composed it brought the first wagons to California and discovered the pass across the Sierra Nevada that serves still as the chief route for railroad, highway, telephone, and airlines. The Donnor Party, however, is of negligible importance historically, but the story has been told and retold, published and republished, because of its dramatic details of starvation, cannibalism, murder, heroism, and disaster. Against every American who knows of the one, a thousand must know of the other. As a kind of final irony, the pass discovered by the Stevens Party has come to be know as Donner Pass.

Yet actually the two parties has much in common. They were groups of Middle Westerners, native and foreign-born, migrating to California. Both included women and children, and traveled overland in oxdrawn covered wagons. Over much of the way they followed the same route. Both were overtaken by winter, and faced their chief difficulties because of snow. Some of the Donner Party spent the winter in a cabin built by three members of the Stevens Party. One individual, Caleb Greenwood, actually figures in both stories.

The difference in the significance, however, springs from two differences in actuality. First, the Stevens Party set out in 1844, two years before the Donner party; they were the trail breakers. Second, the Stevens Party was efficiently run, used good sense, has fairly good luck—in a word, was so successful that it got through without the loss of a single life. The Donner

Party, roughly speaking, was just the opposite, and the upshot was that the casualty list piled up to 42, almost half of the total roster and nearly equaling the whole number of persons in the Stevens Party. The latter, incidentally, arrived in California more numerous by two than at the start because of babies born on the road.

The contrast between the parties is shown even in the nature of the sources of material available on them. No one bothered to record much about the nondramatic Stevens Party, and we should have scarcely any details if it had not been for Moses Schallenberger, a lad of seventeen at the time of the actual events, who forty years later dictated to his schoolmarm daughter his memories of the journey. On the other hand, the story of the Donner Party is possibly the best documented incident of any in the early history of the West. Its dramatic quality was such that everyone and his brother rushed in to tell what he knew about it or thought he knew about it, either at first or second-hand, and publishers took it all.

Of course, this is still the everyday tale. Drive efficiently about your business, and no one ever hears of you. Scatter broken glass and blood over the highway, and a picture of the twisted wreck makes the front page . . .

The Donner Party—to summarize briefly—was formed from family groups of other emigrant parties in July, 1846, and set out by themselves from Little Sandy Creek, in what is now Wyoming, to reach California by the so-called Hastings Route. They lost much time, found the gateway to California blocked by snow, built cabins to winter it out, and ran short of food. Soon they were snowed in deeply, and began to die of starvation. A few escaped across the mountains on improvised snowshoes. Others were saved by the heroic work of rescue parties from the settlements in California. As the result of hardships in the morale of the party degenerated to the point of inhumanity, cannibalism, and possible murder. Of 89 people—men, women, children—involved with the misfortunes of the party, 47 survived, and 42 perished.

The Stevens Party left Council Bluffs of May 18, 1844. Before doing so, they performed what may well have been the act that contributed most to their final success—they elected Elisha Stevens to be their captain.

He was an unusual enough sort of fellow, that Stevens—about forty years old with a big hawk nose and a peaked head; strange-acting, too. He seemed friendly enough, but he was solitary, having his own wagon but neither chick nor child. Born in South Carolina, raised in Georgia, he had trapped in the Rockies for some years, then spent a while in Louisiana, and now finally he was off for California, though no one knows why.

How such a man came to be elected captain is more than can be easily figured out. How did he get more votes than big-talking Dr. John Townsend, the only member of the party with professional status and of some education? Or more than Martin Murphy, Jr., who could muster kinsmen and fellow Irishmen numerous enough to make up a majority of votes? Perhaps Stevens has a compromise candidate between the native American and the Irish contingents that split the party and might well have brought quarrels and disaster. He had good experience behind him, indeed. And perhaps there was something about him that marked him for the natural leader of men that he apparently was. His election seems to me one of those events giving rise to the exclamation, "It makes you believe in democracy!"

Yes, he took the Wagons through. If there were justice in history, his name would stand on the pass he found and conquered, and not merely on a little creek that runs into San Francisco Bay.

So they pushed off from the Missouri River that spring day, numbering 26 men, eight women, and about seventeen children. During the first part of the journey they traveled in company with a larger party bound for Oregon. The swollen Elkhorn River blocked the way, but they emptied the wagons, ferried everything across in a waterproofed wagon bed, swam the cattle, and kept ahead. They chased buffalo, saw their first wild Indians at Fort Laramie. At Independence Rock they halted a week to rest the oxen, "make meat" by hunting buffalo, and allow Helen Independence Miller to be born. They were the first to take wagons across the Green River Desert by what was later known as Sublette's (or Greenwood's) cutoff. On the cutoff they suffered from thirst, had their cattle stampede (but got them back), were scared by a Sioux war party (but had no real trouble). All this, of course, is mere routine for a covered wagon journey, nothing to make copy of.

At Fort Hall they separated from the Oregon party. At Raft River, eleven wagons in the line, they left the Oregon Trail, and headed south and west, following the wheel tracks of an emigrant party that Joe Walker, the famous mountain man, had tried to take to California the year before. Whether the people in the Stevens Party knew of his failure— the people got through, but the wagons were abandoned—is only one of the many details we do not know. Uneventfully and monotonously they followed his trail all the way to Humboldt Sink, a matter of 500 miles. Then, after careful scouting and on the advice of an intelligent Paiute chief, whom they called Truckee, they decided to quit following Walker and strike west.

From that point they were on their own, making history by breaking trail for the forty-niners, the Central Pacific, and U.S. 40. They made it across the Forty-Mile Desert with less trouble than might have been expected, considering that they were the first. Even so, the crossing took 48 hours, and the oxen were thirst-crazed by the time they approached the cottonwoods marking the line of a stream. The men of the party, with their usual good sense, unyoked the oxen some distance from the stream to prevent them from scenting water while still attached to the wagons and stampeding toward it. Thankful to their guide, the emigrants named the stream the Truckee, and prudently camped two days among its cottonwoods for rest and recuperation.

They knew no route, except to follow the river. The canyon got tighter and tighter until in places they merely took their wagons upstream like river boats. The oxen began to give out, hoofs softening because of being in the water so much. Now it came November, and a foot of snow fell. The oxen would have starved except for some tall rushes growing along the water.

Finally they came to where the river forked. Which way to go? They held "a consultation," which must have been close to a council of desperation. it was past the middle of November—snow two feet deep now, high mountain crags in view ahead, oxen footsore and gaunt, food low, womenfolks getting scared. But they were good men and staunch. They must have been—or we would have had the Donner story two years earlier.

Yes, there must have been some good men, and we know the names, if not much else about them. Old Caleb Greenwood the trapper was there, and he would have been heard with respect, though personally I do not cast him for the hero's part, as some do. Neither do I have much confidence in "Doc" Townsend, though his name is sometimes used to identify the whole party; he was full of wild ideas. But "Young" Martin Murphy, Irish as his name, was probably a good man, and so, I think, was Dennis Martin, Irish too. Then there was Hitchcock, whose Christian name has been lost because everyone has referred to him just as "Old Man" Hitchcock; he should have been valuable in the council, having been a mountain man in his day. But the one on whom I put my money is Stevens himself, who had taken them all the way, so far, without losing a man.

He or some other, or all of them together, worked out the plan, and it came out in the end as what we would call today a calculated risk, with a certain hedging of the bets. Leave five wagons below the pass at what is now called Donner Lake, and three young men with them, volunteers, to build a cabin and guard the wagons and goods through the winter. Take six wagons ahead over the pass, and with them the main body including all the mothers and children. Up the other fork of the river, send a party of two women and four men, all young, well-mounted and well-armed, prepared to travel light and fast and live off the country. unencumbered they can certainly make it through somewhere; when they get to Sutter's Fort, they can have help sent back, if necessary.

So Captain Stevens and the main body took to six wagons ahead to the west, and with a heave and a ho, in spite of sheer granite ledges and ever-deepening snow, they hoisted those wagons up the pass, which is really not a pass so much as the face of a mountain. Even today, when you view those granite slopes, close to precipices, and imagine taking wagons up through the snow, it seems incredible.

Beyond the pass, some days' journey, they got snowed in, but by that time they were over the worst. On Yuba River they built a cabin to winter it out, and Elizabeth Yuba Murphy was born there. Eventually all of them, including E. Y. M., together with the wagons, got safely through to Sutter's.

As for the light-cavalry unit that took the others fork, they went up the stream, were the first white people of record to stand on the shore of Lake Tahoe, then turned west across the mountains. They suffered hardship, but got through.

That brings everybody in except the three young men who were with the wagons at the lake. They had built themselves a cabin, and were just settling down to enjoy a pleasant winter of hunting in the woods when snow started falling. Before long, the cabin was up to the eaves, all game had disappeared, no man could walk. The three were left with two starving cows that they slaughtered, but they themselves were soon close to starving. They decided to et out of there fast, and so manufactured themselves crude snowshoes of the hickory strips that held up the canvases on the covered wagons.

One morning they set out—each with ten pounds of dried beef, rifle and ammunition, and two blankets. The snow was light and powdery, ten feet deep. The improvised snow-shoes were heavy and clumsy, and exhausting to use. By evening the three had reached the summit of the pass, but young Moses Schallenberger, a mere gawky lad of seventeen, was sick and exhausted.

In the morning he realized that he could not make it through. Rather than impede his companions, he said good-by and turned back—with no expectation but death. The two others went on, and reached Sutter's Fort.

All in now but Moses Schallenberger! He had barely managed to make it back, col-lapsing at the very cabin and having to drag himself over the doorsill. He felt a little better the next day, forced himself to go out hunting on his snowshoes, saw nothing except fox tracks. Back at the cabin, "discouraged and sick at heart," he happened to notice some traps that Captain Stevens had left behind.

Next day he set traps, and during the night caught a coyote. He tried eating it, but found the flesh revolting, no matter how cooked. Still, he managed to live on that meat for three days, and they found two foxes in the traps. To his delight, the fox meat was deli-cious. This was about the middle of December. From then on, he managed to trap foxes and coyotes. He lived on the former, and hung the latter up to freeze, always fearing that he would have to eat another one, but keeping them as a reserve.

Alone in the snow-buried cabin, through the dim days and long nights of midwinter, week after week, assailed by fierce storms, often despairing of his life, he suffered from deep depression. As he put it later, "My life was more miserable than I can describe," but he never lost the will to live. Fortunately he found some books that "Doc" Townsend had been taking to California, and reading became his solace. The two works that he later men-tioned as having pored over were the poems of Byron, and (God save the mark!) the letters of Lord Chesterfield.

Thus the boy lived on, despondent but resolute, eating the foxes and hanging up his coyotes until he had a line of eleven of them. The weeks dragged along until it was the end of February, and still the snow was deep and the mountain winter showed no sign of break-ing. Then, one evening a little before sunset, he was standing near the cabin, and suddenly saw someone approaching. At first he imagined it to be an Indian, but then he recognized his old comrade Dennis Martin!

Martin had traveled a long road since he went over the pass with the main body, in the middle of November. He had been picked up in the twirl of a California revolution and marched south almost to Los Angeles. Returning, he had heard of Schallenberger's being left behind, and had come across the pass on snowshoes to see if he were still alive to be rescued.

Martin had lived for some years in Canada, and was an expert on snowshoes. He made a good pair for Schallenberger, and taught him their use. Thus aided, the lad made it over the pass without great difficulty. The last one was through!

The men of the party even went back the next summer, and brought out the wagons that had been left east of the pass. The only loss was their contents, taken by wandering Indians, except for the firearms, which the Indians considered bad medicine . . .

If we return to the story that offers natural comparison with that of the Steven Party, we must admit that the historical significance of the Donnor Party is negligible. The road that the Donners cut through the Wasatch Mountains was useful to the Mormons when they settled by Great Salt Lake, but they would have got through without it. The Donnors served as a kind of horrible example to later emigrants, and so may have helped to prevent other such covered wagon disasters. That is about all that can be totaled up.

There is, of course, no use arguing. The Donner Party has what it takes for a good story, even a dog—everything, you might say, except young love. So, when I drive past the massive bronze statue of the Donner Memorial and up over the pass, I think of these folk who endured and struggled, and died or lived, to produce what may be called the story of stories of the American frontier.

But as I drive over the pass, fighting the summer traffic of U.S. 40 or the winter blizzard, I also like to remember those earlier ones, to think of hawk-nosed Elisha Stevens; of Caleb Greenwood and "Old Man" Hitchcock; or gawky Moses Schallenberger, letting his comrades go on and facing death; of Mrs. Townsend, Moses' sister, riding her Indian pony with the horseback party; of Martin Murphy and fantastic "Doc" Townsend; of Dennis Martin who knew about snowshoes.

These are the ones who discovered the pass and took the wagons over, who kept out of emergencies or had the wit and strength to overcome them, who did not make a good story by getting into trouble, but made history by keeping out of trouble.

The Great Oneida Love-in

Morris Bishop

Sin, the conviction of sin, the assurance of punishment for sin, pervaded pioneer American like the fever and ague, and took nearly as many victims. Taught that in Adam's fall we had sinned all, threatened with hell-fire by revivalist preachers, tortured by the guilt of intimate offenses, earnest youths whipped themselves into madness and suicide, and died crying that they had committed the sin against the Holy Ghost, which is unforgivable, though no one knows quite what it is.

The year 1831 was known as the Great Rivival, when itinerant evangelists powerfully shook the bush and gathered in a great harvest of sinners. In September of that year John Humphrey Noyes, a twenty-year-old Dartmouth graduate and a law student in Putney, Vermont, attended such a revival. He was in a mood of metaphysical despair, aggravated by a severe cold. During the exhortings the conviction of salvation came to him. Light gleamed upon his soul. "Ere the day was done," he wrote later, "I had concluded to devote myself to the service and ministry of God."

Noyes was a young man of good family. His father was a Dartmouth graduate, a successful merchant in Putney, and a congressman. John was a bookish youth, delighting in history, romance, and poetry of a martial character, such as lives of Napoleon or of the Crusaders or Sir Walter Scott's *Marmion*. He was red-haired and freckled, and thought himself too homely ever to consider marriage. But when he began preaching his face shone like an angel's; one of his sons later averred that "there was about him an unmistakable and somewhat unexpected air of spiritual assurance." According to his phrenologi-

17

cal analysis, his bumps of amativeness, combativeness, and self-esteem were large, his benevolence and philoprogenitiveness very large. His life confirmed these findings.

After his mystical experience in Putney, Noyes spent a year in the Andover Theological Seminary (Congregational). He found his teachers and companions lukewarm in piety, and devoted himself to an intensive study of the new Testament, most of which he could recite by heart. A divine direction—"I know that ye seek Jesus which was crucified. He is not here"—sent him from Andover to the Yale Theological Seminary in New Haven. There he came in contact with the doctrine of perfectionism and was allured by it.

Perfectionism asserted with men may be freed from sin and attain in this life the perfect holiness necessary to salvation. It rejected therefore the consequences of original sin and went counter to the Calvinistic dogma of total depravity. Perfectionism took shape early in the nineteenth century and found lodgment among adventurous groups in New Haven, Newark, Albany, and in villages of central New York, "the burned-over district," where religion smote with a searing flame. Perfectionism was likely to develop into antinomianism, the contention that the faithful are "directly infused with the holy spirit" and thus free from the claims and obligations of Old Testament moral law. And antinomianism led readily to scandal, as when three perfectionist missionaries, two men and a sister of one of them, were tarred and feathered for sleeping together in one bed.

Though suspected of perfectionist heresy, Noyes was licensed to preach in August, 1833. At about the same time, he made a sensational discovery: Jesus Christ had announced that He would return during the lifetime of some of His disciples. Jesus could not have been mistaken; therefore the Second Coming of Christ had taken place in A.D. 70. The "Jewish cycle" of religious history then ended and a "Gentile cycle" began, in which the Church has improperly usurped the authority of the apostles. We live no longer in an age of prophecy and promise, but in an age of fulfillment. Perfect holiness is attainable in this life, as well as guaranteed deliverance from sin.

Noyes found this revelation by fasting, prayer, and diligent search of the Scriptures. At divine command he announced it in a sermon to the Free Church of New Haven on February 20, 1834. "I went home with a feeling that I had committed myself irreversibly, and on my bed that night I received the baptism which I desired and expected. Three times in quick succession a stream of eternal love gushed through my heart, and rolled back again to its source. 'Joy unspeakable and full of glory' filled my soul. All fear and doubt and condemnation passed away. I knew that my heart was clean, and that the Father and the Son had come and made it their abode."

This was all very well, but next day the word ran through New Haven, "Noyes says he is perfect!" with the inevitable corollary, "Noyes is crazy!" The authorities promptly expelled him from the seminary and revoked his license to preach. But the perfect are proof against imperfect human detractors. "I have taken away their license to sin, and they keep on sinning," said Noyes. "So, though they have taken away my license to preach, I shall keep on preaching." This he did, with some success. His first convert was Miss Abigail Merwin of Orange, Connecticut, with whom he felt himself sealed in the faith.

Nevertheless his way was far from smooth. He had yet to pass through what he called "the dark valley of conviction." He went to New York and wandered the streets in a kind of frenzy, catching a little sleep by lying down in a doorway, or on the steps of City Hall, or on a bench at the Battery. He sought the most ill-famed regions of the city. "I descended into cellars where abandoned men and women were gathered, and talked familiarly with them about their ways of life, beseeching them to believe on Christ, that they might be save from their sins. They listened to me without abuse." Tempted by the Evil One, he doubted all, even the Bible, even Christ, even Abigail Merwin, whom he suspected to be Satan in angelic disguise. But after drinking the dregs of the cup of trembling he merged purified and secure. He retreated to Putney for peace and shelter. His friends, even his sister, thought him deranged. But such was the power of his spirit that he gathered a little group of adepts, relatives, and friends to accept his revelation.

Miss Abigail Merwin, however, took fright, married a schoolteacher, and removed to Ithaca, New York. Noyes followed her there—a rather ungentlemanly procedure. After a few months she left her husband, but not Noyes's arms—only to return to her father in Connecticut.

Noyes was delight with the pretty village of Ithaca, with his lodging in the Clinton House, and especially with the broad-minded printers, unafraid of publishing heresies and liberal with credit. On August 20, 1837, he established a periodical, the *Witness,* for a subscription rate of one dollar, or, if a dollar should be inconvenient, for nothing. The issue of September 23 reverberated far beyond the subscription list of faithful perfectionists. Noyes had written a private letter expressing his radical views on marriage among the perfect. By a violation of confidence, this had reached the free-thinking editor of a paper called the *Battle-Axe.* Noyes, disdaining evasion, acknowledged in the *Witness* his authorship of the letter and reiterated his starling conclusions. The essential of "the *Battle-Axe* letter" lies in the concluding words: "When the will of God is done on earth as it is in heaven, *there will be no marriage.* The marriage supper of the Lamb is a feast at which *every dish is free to every guest.* Exclusiveness, jealousy, quarreling, have no place there, for the same reason as that which forbids the guests at a thanksgiving dinner to claim each his separate dish, and quarrel with the rest for his rights. In a holy community, there is no more reason why sexual intercourse should be restrained by law, than why eating and drinking should be— and there is as little occasion for shame in the one as in the other. . . . The guests of the marriage supper may each have his favorite dish, each dish of his own procuring, and that without the jealousy of exclusiveness."

Ungallant as this statement is in its characterization of women as dishes to pass, it states a reasonable protest against the egotisms of marriage. One may readily perceive in it also a secret resentment against the unfaithful Abigail Merwin. One may even interpret it as the erotic outburst of repressed impulse. Noyes, an impassioned, amorous type, and still a virgin.

Noyes was soon vouchsafed a sign, almost a miracle. When he was eighty dollars in debt to an Ithaca printer, he was eighty dollars in debt to an Ithaca printer, he received from a disciple in Vermont, Miss Harriet A. Holton of Westminster, a letter enclosing a gift of exactly eight dollars. He paid his bill, returned to Putney, and after a decent interval, forgetting the perfectionist views of the *Battle-Axe* letter, proposed exclusive marriage to Miss Holton. The two were formally united in Chesterfield, New Hampshire, on June 28, 1938. For a honeymoon they drove to Albany to buy a second-hand printing press, with more of Harriet's money.

Thus began the Putney Community, which at first consisted only of Noyes and his wife, several of his brothers and sisters, and a small cluster of converts from the neighborhood. They lived in a group, sharing possessions and duties. Their chief occupations were spiritual exercises in pursuit of holiness and the printing of the *Witness* on their own press. Noyes had no great liking for sheer honest toil for its own sake; he wished to secure for all the freedom for spiritual development. The women prepared one hot meal a day—breakfast. Thereafter the hungry had to help themselves in the kitchen.

Noyes was restless in the monotonous peace of Putney. His wife inherited $9,000 in 1844; Noyes was provoked to fantastic visions. He wrote his wife: "In order to subdue the world to Christ we must carry religion into money-making." He proposed first a theological seminary for perfectionism, then agencies in Boston and New York to distribute their spiritual goods. "Then we must advance into foreign commerce, and as our means enlarge we must cover the ocean with our ships and the whole world with the knowledge of Go. This is a great scheme, but not too great or God. . . . Within ten years we will plant the standard of Christ on the highest battlements of the world."

Though allured by such shimmering visions, he had to deal with present problems. An urgent personal problem was that of sex. His wife was pregnant five times in six years. She endured long agonies ending in four stillbirths. The only surviving child was Theodore, born in 1841. John Noyes suffered with his wife, and he protested against cruel nature, perhaps against God. Surely women were not made to suffer so. Surely there was a better way. A perfectionist could not brook flagrant imperfection. Noyes's habit was to seek and find a better way, and then sanctify it. The better way turned out to be male continence.

Noyes had been trained in the Puritan ethic, which did not regard marital sex as unholy. Nevertheless the consequences of male egotism horrified him. "It is as foolish and cruel to expend one's seed on a wife merely for the sake of getting rid of it," he wrote, "as it would be to fire a gun at one's best friend merely for the sake of unloading it." After his wife's disasters he lived for a time chaste by her side. But chastity proving to be no solution at all, he embraced male continence, of which the definition embarrasses the chaste pen. When embarrassed, the chaste pen may decently quote. One of the community disciples, H. J. Seymour, thus defined the practice: "checking the flow of amative passion before it reaches the point of exposing the man to the loss of virile energy, or the woman to the danger of undesired child-bearing." Or, with Latin decorum, *coitus reservatus;* or, ore colloquially, everything but.

This was not actually the beginning of birth-control advocacy. In 1832 a Boston physician, Charles Knowlton, published *The Fruits of Philosophy; or the Private Companion of Young Married People,* pointing to the menace of excessive child-bearing and eventual overpopulation, and recommending contraception. Dr. Knowlton and his publisher were accused of blasphemy. Their case was carried to the Supreme Court, and they were condemned to several months in jail. Robert Dale Owen, the reformer of New Harmony, Indiana, supported by Miss Frances Wright, "the Priestess of Beelzebub," carried on the work. In his *Moral Physiology* (1836), Owen recommended *coitus interruptus,* which Noyes scored as substituting self-indulgence for self-control.

"Amativeness is to life as sunshine is to vegetation," wrote Noyes twelve years later in his *Bible Argument Defining the Relation of the Sexes in the Kingdom of Heaven.* "Ordinary sexual intercourse (in which the amative and propagative functions are confounded) is a momentary affair, terminating in exhaustion and disgust. . . . Adam and Eve . . . sunk the spiritual in the sensual in their intercourse with each other, by pushing prematurely beyond the amative to the propagative, and so became ashamed." In the future society, "as propagation will become one of the 'fine arts.' Indeed it will rank above music, painting, sculpture, &c.; for it combines the charms and the benefits of them all."

All this is very noble and high-minded; but we are trained to look for—and we usually find—a casuistical serpent in the gardens, who is able to transform impulse into ideals, even into new theologies. The serpent in this case was Mary Cragin, who with her husband, George, had joined the Putney Community. Mary was a charmer, and, to put it baldly, sexy. (Do not condemn her; some are, some aren't. This is a well-known fact.) Noyes feared that she might "become a Magdalene" if he did not save her. One evening in the woods, Noyes and Mary discovered that they were united by a deep spiritual bond. "We took some liberty of embracing, and Mrs. George distinctly gave me to understand that she was ready for the full consummation." But Noyes insisted on a committee meeting with the respective spouses. "We gave each other full liberty, and so entered into marriage in guartette form. The last part of the interview was as amiable and happy as a wedding, and a full consummation . . . followed."

This was Noyes's first infidelity, according to the world's idiom. He found a more grandiloquent term for it—complex marriage, to contrast with the restrictiveness of simple marriage. Heaven beamed on the participants. "Our love is of God; it is destitute of exclusiveness, each one rejoicing in the happiness of the others," said Mary. The Putney Community, in general, applauded; some, under direction, adopted the new cure for marital selfishness. It appears that some puritan wives, as well as husbands, were secretly weary of the "scanty and monotonous fare" provided by monogamy.

But righteous Putney soon had hints of the goings-on and uprose in anger. On October 26, 1847, Noyes was arrested, charged with adultery, and released, pending trial, in $2,000 bail. Noyes declared himself guiltless, insisting that in common law no tort has been committed if no one is injured. "The head and front and whole of our offense is communism of love. . . . If this is the unpardonable sin in the world, we are sure it is the beauty and glory of heaven." But in fear of mob violence from "the barbarians of Putney" he thought it well to jump bail, following the counsel of the highest authority: "When they persecute you in this city, flee ye into another."

A refuge awaited the persecuted saints in the burned-over district of central New York, a region familiar to Noyes. A group of perfectionists offered the Putneyans a sawmill and forty acres of woodland on Oneida Creek, halfway between Syracuse and Utica. It was a bland, fertile, welcoming country, suitable for an Eden. By good omen, the spot was the exact geographical center of New York, if one overlooked Long Island.

In mid-February of 1848, "the year of the great change," the pilgrims began to arrive. Defying the upstate winter, lodging in abandoned cabins, they set to with a will to build a community dwelling and workshops. Some of the neighbors looked at them askance; most welcomed these honest, pious, industrious newcomers, and some even were converted to perfectionism and threw in their lot with the colony,

The early years were the heroic age of Oneida. All worked together, cutting and sawing timber, digging clay for bricks, building simple houses, clearing land for vegetable gardens. Everyone took his or her turn at the household tasks. All work was held in equal honor, without prestige connotations. Noyes recognized that most American experiments in communal life had foundered because they were established on the narrow base of agriculture; his communism world live on industry. Thus Oneida marketed canned fruits and vegetables, sewing silk, straw hats, mop sticks, travelling bags, and finally, silver tableware. Its traps for animals, from rodents to bears, become famous as far as Alaska and Siberia. The cruelty of traps seldom occurred to the makers, who were frontiersmen as well as perfectionists. Sympathy with suffering beasts and the conservation of wildlife were concepts still undeveloped. To a critic, Noyes replied that since God had to cleanse it. Salesmen, known only as peddlers, were sent out to market the wares. On their return, they were given a Turkish bath and a sharp examination on faith and practice, a spiritual rubdown to expunge the stains of the unregenerative world.

The Oneida Community prospered. The numbers of the faithful rose. The great Mansion House, the community home, was begun in 1860 and completed a dozen years later. It is a far-wandering red-brick building or group of buildings, standing on a knoll amid magnificient fat trees. Harmoniously proportioned, with its towers, mansard roofs, and tall French windows, it is a superb example of mid-nineteenth-century architecture. Its message is security, peace, and material comfort. The interior is graced with fine woodwork and decorations. The parlors, the excellent library, the lovely assembly hall, are redolent with memories, jealously preserved and proudly recounted. Here live a number of descendants of the original Oneidans, together with some lodgers, still regarded with kindly pity as "foreign bodies."

The memories, second-hand though they are, are all of a happy time, of a golden age long lost. John Humphrey Noyes, affectionately referred to by his grandchildren as "the Honorable John," was a cheerful person, and imposed happiness on his great family. The story is told of a visitor who asked her guide: "What is the fragrance I smell here in this house?" The guide answered: "It may be the odor of crushed selfishness." There was no money within the Oneida economy, no private possession, no competition for food and shelter, and hence little rivalry.

All worked and played together. Whenever possible, work was done on the "bee" system; thus a party of men and women would make handbags on the law, while a dramatic voice read a novel aloud. Glasses were conducted in such recondite subjects as Greek and Hebrew. Dances and respectable card games, like euchre and whist, were in favor. Amateur theatricals were a constant diversion. The productions of *The Merchant of Venice, The Merry Wives of Windsor,* and especially of *H.M.S. Pinafore,* were famous as far as Utica and Syracuse. Music was encouraged, with an orchestra and much vocalization. Music, Noyes mused, was closely related to sexual love; it was an echo of the passions. However, music contained a menace; it gave rise to rivalries, jealousies, and vanities, to what Noyes reproved as "prima donna fever."

Noyes had strong views on dress. He called the contrast of men's and women's costumes immodest, in that it proclaimed the distinction of sex. "In a state of nature, the difference between a man and a woman could hardly be distinguished at a distance of five hundred yards, but as men and women dress, their sex is telegraphed as far as they can be seen. Woman's dress is a standing lie. It proclaims that she is not a two-legged animal, but something like a churn, standing on castors. . . . Gowns operate as shackles, and they are put on that sex which has most talent in the legs."

From the beginning of Oneida, a new dress for women was devised, loose skirts to the knee with pantalets below, thus approximating a gentleman's frock coat and trousers. Some visitors were shocked, some were amused; few were allured. Indeed, the specimens remaining in the community's collections and the representations in photographs hardly seem beautiful. But the wearers rejoiced in their new freedom of movement. They cut their hair, in despite of Saint Paul. It was asserted they looked and felt younger.

For thirty years the community, a placid island amid the stormy seas of society, lived its insulated life. It numbered, at its peak, three hundred members. It was undisturbed, except by invasions of visitors brought on bargain excursions by the railroads. As many as a thousand appeared on a single day, picnicking on the grounds, invading the workshops and private quarters. They were welcomed; but on their departure all the Oneidans turned to in order to collect the scatterings, to scrub out the tobacco stains on the parquet floors.

The structure, the doctrine, the persistence of Oneida made a unique social phenomenon. It was consciously a family, with Noyes as father. As Constance Noyes Robertson says, it substituted "for the small unit of home and family and individual possessions the larger unit of group-family and group-family life." Its faith was "Bible Communism." Though it held aloof from all churches and deconsecrated the Sabbath, it was pietistic in demanding the regeneration of society by rejecting competition, a money economy, and private ownership, whether of goods or persons. But it was not Marxian, for it made no mention of class warfare, of a revolution to come, of proletarian dictatorship.

The internal organization of the community was loose and vague, depending largely on the will of Noyes. Justice and discipline were administered informally, if at all. To provide correction, Noyes trusted chiefly to a procedure known as mutual criticism. Saint Paul had said: "Speak every man truth with his neighbor; for we are members one of another"; and the Apostle James: "Confess your faults one to another." When an individual offered himself for criticism, or was designated from above, a committee prepared his "trial," but any member might join in the proceedings. The trial was a game, though a serious one. The subject was informed of his secret faults, of shortcomings he had not suspected. He learned that his very virtues, on which he had flattered himself, were only disguised vices. The critics would pounce on an unpopular fellow-member with glee, seizing the opportunity to reveal to him some home truths, at the same time revealing their hidden rancors. A transcript of the proceedings was posted and often printed. The subject of this primitive psychoanalysis was likely to suffer dreadfully from his new self-knowledge. "I was metaphorically stood upon my head and allowed to drain until all the self-righteousness had dripped out of me." Afterward the subject felt enlightened, purified, happy. "Mutual criticism," said Noyes, "subordinates the I-spirit to the We-spirit." It also made the subjects, mostly brooding introspectives, for a time the center of interest and concern for the whole community. Mutual criticism, under the name of "krinopathy," was even used as a therapeutic device to cure children's colds, with, it was said, remarkable success.

Of the various Oneida institutions, the most fascinating to the prurient observer is the organization of sex behavior. Since the community was a single great family, there could be within it no marrying and giving in marriage. Each was married to all, Noyes insisted; every man was husband and brother to every woman. Love, far from being a sin, was holy, a sacrament; in the sexual experience one escaped from egotism and selfhood into the ecstasy of communion. Every effort must be to "abound"—one of Noyes's favorite words. One must spend, not hoard. The human heart seldom realizes its possibilities; it "is capable of loving any number of times and any number of persons; the more it loves the more it can love." One had only to look at surrounding society to recognize the evils of exclusive marriage, the chains binding unmatched natures, the secret adulteries, actual or of the heart, the hate-filled divorces, women's disease, prostitution, masturbation, licentiousness in general.

Noyes maintained that sexual love was not naturally restricted to pairs, and second marriages were often the happiest. "Men and women find universally (however the fact may be concealed) that their susceptibility to love is not burned out by one honeymoon, or satisfied by one lover." The body should assert its rights; religion should make use of the senses as helpers of devotion. Sexual shame, the consequence of the fall of man, was factitious and irrational. "Shame ought to be banished from the company of virtue, though in the world it has stolen the very name of virtue. . . . Shame gives rise to the theory that sexual offices have no place in heaven. Anyone who has true modesty would sooner banish singing from heaven than sexual music." Beware, said Noyes, of one who proclaims that he is free from sexual desire, beware of religious teachers with fondling hands. Beware especially of Dr. Josiah Gridley of Southamptom. Massachusetts, who boasts that he could carry a virgin in each hand without the least stir of passion. In short, "you must not serve the lusts of the flesh; if you do you will be damned. You must not make monks of yourself; if you do you will be damned."

One might suspect that these doctrines would have led to outright antinomianism and to general orgies. Nothing of the sort occurred, thanks to the watchful care of Noyes and thanks to the character of the Oneidans, devout and rather humorless seekers for perfection. The system of complex marriage, or pantagamy, begun in Putney, was instituted. A man might request the privilege of a private visit with a lady, or a lady might take the initiative, for "in all nature the female element invites and the male responds." The request was submitted to a committee of elders, headed by Noyes, who gave the final approval or disapproval. The mate besought had the right of refusal. It was recommended that older women initiate young men, and vice versa. Thus the young men were expertly guided in the practice of male continence, while the maturer men undertook without complaint the education of the maidens. The committee was also concerned to break up "exclusive and idolatrous attachments" of two persons of the same age, for these bred selfishness. We are assured that complex marriage worked admirably, and that for many life became a continuous courtship. "Amativeness, the lion of the tribe of human passions, is conquered and civilized among us." But the records are unwontedly reticent on the details of the system's operation. Only one scandal is remembered, when an unworthy recruit tried to force his attentions on the women, and was expelled through a window into a snowdrift. One suspects that in spite of all the spiritual training, there were heartaches and hidden anger, and much whispering and giggling at the sound of midnight footsteps on the stairs.

The flaw in the system of continence was the threatening sterilization of the movement—the fate of the Shakers. Noyes recognized the danger, and in his *Bible Argument* of 1848 had proposed scientific propagation to replace random or involuntary propagation. But the time was not yet ripe. In the difficult early years of Oneida, Noyes discouraged childbearing, and his docile followers produced only forty-four offspring in twenty years. Then increasing prosperity permitted him to take steps for the perpetuation of his community. Early in 1869, he proposed the inauguration of stirpiculture, or the scientific improvement of the human stock by breeding. "Every race-horse, every straight-backed bull, every premium pig tells us what we can do and what we must do for men." Oneida should be a laboratory for the preparation of the great race of the future.

The Oneidans, especially the younger ones, greeted the proposal with enthusiasm. Fifty-three young women signed these resolutions:

1. That we do not belong to ourselves in any respect, but that we do belong to *God*, and second to Mr. Noyes as God's true representative.
2. That we have no rights or personal feelings in regard to childbearing which shall in the least degree oppose or embarrass him in his choice of scientific combinations.
3. That we will put aside all envy, childishness and self-seeking, and rejoice with those who are chosen candidates; that we will, if necessary, become martyrs to science, and cheerfully resign all desire to become mothers, if for any reason Mr. Noyes deem us unfit material for propagation. Above all, we offer ourselves "living sacrifices" to God and true Communism.

At the same time thirty-eight young men made a corresponding declaration to Noyes:

The undersigned desire you may feel that we most heartily sympathize with your purpose in regard to scientific propagation, and offer ourselves to be used in forming any combinations that may seem to you desirable. We claim no rights. We ask no privileges. We desire to be servants of the truth. We ask no privileges. We desire to be servants of the truth. With a prayer that the grace of God will help us in this resolution, we are your true soldiers.

Thus began the first organized experiment in human eugenics. For several years Noyes directed all the matings, on the basis of physical, spiritual, moral, and intellectual suitability. In 1875 a committee of six men and six women was formed to issue licenses to propagate. The selective process bore some bitter fruit. The eliminated males particularly were unhappy, unconsoled by the reflection that in animal breeding one superior stud may serve many females. Noyes relented in his scientific purpose so far as to permit one child to each male applicant. There was also some covert grumbling that Noyes, then in his sixties, elected himself to father nine children, by several mates. Eugenically, to be sure, he was entirely justified; there could be no doubt of his superiority.

The results of the stirpicultural experiment have not been scientifically studied, though an article by Hilda Herrick Noyes, prepared in 1921, offered some valuable statistical information. About one hundred men and women took part; eight-one became parents, producing fifty-eight living children and four stillborn. No mothers were lost during the experiment; no defective children were produced. The health of the offspring was exceptionally good; their longevity has far surpassed the average expectations of life. The children, and the children's children, constitute a very superior group, handsome and intelligent. Many have brilliantly conducted the affairs of their great manufacturing corporations; others have distinguished themselves in public service, the arts, and literature.

The integration of the children into the community caused some difficulties. The mother kept her child until he was weaned and could walk, then he was transferred to the Children's House, though he might return to his mother for night care. Noyes, with his ideal of the community family, disapproved of egotistic, divisive "special love"; the mothers were permitted to see their children only once or twice a week. The children were excellently educated in the nursery school, the kindergarten, and the grammar school, by teachers chosen for their competence and natural liking for the young. If the children cried for their mothers, they were severely reproved for "partiality" or "stickiness." One graduate of the Children's House remembered that when he was forbidden to visit his mother he went berserk. Another recalled her agony when she caught sight of her mother after a fortnight's enforced separation. The child begged her mother not to leave her—and the mother fled for fear of a penalty of an additional week's separation from her child.

The atmosphere of the Children's House was, in short, that of a friendly orphanage. If the disruption of the family units had any bad psychic effects on the children, they have not been recorded. Children accept their world as it is; they know no other. The memories of the Oneida boys and girls are mostly of happy schooldays under kind teachers, days of laughter, play, and delightful learning. The judgment of on eminent product, Pierrepont B.

Noyes, is surely correct, that the community system was harder on the mothers than on the children.

The fathers were more remote from their children than were the mothers. Pierrepont Noyes admitted: "Father never seemed a father to me in the ordinary sense." The system reflected indeed the character of John Humphrey Noyes. He was the Father of his people, the semidivine begetter of a community, and he loved the community communally. He saw no reason to encourage family bonds, "partiality," among the faithful, at cost to the community spirit. He seems to have shown little personal affection for his sons after the flesh. No doubt a phrenologist would have noted that his bump of parental love was small. One is tempted to go further, to see in his disregard for his children a certain horror of paternity, a deep-implanted remembrance of his four stillborn babies, of his wife's sufferings and his own.

The rumors of strange sex practices roused the righteous and the orthodox, already angered by Oneida's nonobservance of the Sabbath and rejection of church affiliations. A professor at Hamilton College, John W. Mears, still the bogeyman of Oneida after a hundred years, began in 1873 a long campaign to destroy the community and its band of sinners. Though most of the inhabitants and newspaper editors of the region defended Noyes and his followers, though local justice could find no grounds for prosecution, the churches demanded action against "the ethics of the barnyard," and sought enabling legislation from the state. The menace mounted until, in June, 1879, Noyes fled to Canada, as, thirty-one years before, he had fled from Vermont. From a new home in Niagara Falls, Ontario, he continued to advise and inspire his old companions until his death, on April 13, 1886.

With the Father's departure the community system collapsed. In August, 1879, complex marriage was abandoned. Most of the Oneidans paired off and married, to legitimize their children. There were distressing cases of mothers whose mates were already taken, of the children of Noyes himself, left high and dry. In the reorganization into conventional families, it was necessary to establish rights of private property. As Noyes had foreseen, the demons of greed, self-seeking, jealousy, anger, and uncharitableness invaded the serene halls of the Mansion House.

The Oneida industries were converted into a joint-stock company, the shares distributed to the members of the community. After a period of drifting and fumbling, the widely varied enterprises came under the inspired management of Pierrepont Noyes and became models of welfare capitalism, or the partnership of owners and workers. To the present day, high wages are paid, profits are shared, schools, country clubs, aids for home-building, are provided. Oneida is the leading producer of stainless-steel flatware, the second largest producer of silver-plated ware in the United States. It has over three thousand employees in the Oneida plants, and many more in the factories in Canada, Mexico, and the United Kingdom. Its net sales in 1967 amounted to fifty-four million dollars, with net profits of two and a half million.

This outcome is not the least surprising feature of the Oneida story. Nearly all other communistic experiments in this country have long since disappeared, leaving nothing more than a tumble-down barracks or a roadside marker. Oneida found a transformation into the capitalist world. It did so at the cost of losing its religious and social doctrines; but it has never lose the idealism, the humanitarianism, and the communitarian love of John Humphrey Noyes.

"The Gray-Eyed Man of Destiny"

Edward S. Wallace

For a young American who wanted excitement and adventure along with a chance to get rich quick, the United States of a hundred years ago offered plentiful opportunity. The adjustment of the Oregon boundary with Great Britain in 1846, the decisive victory over Mexico and the acquisition of about half the territory of that unfortunate republic in 1848, and then, almost immediately afterward, the discovery of gold in California—all these opened avenues of adventure for men of mettle and daring.

There was, as well, for the truly reckless or the desperate, an even more alluring outlet than settling new lands or prospecting for gold, and this had the promise that the gold they were after had already been mined. The men who followed this highly dangerous way were called filibusters—a term used then in its most masculine sense, meaning freebooters, and not, as now, windy and obstructive politicians. These exuberant daredevils tried to seize by force of arms various Latin American countries, usually with the sincere belief that they were the instruments of the "Manifest Destiny" of the United States to acquire and civilize the chaotic and wartorn republics to the south.

The extremists of this imperialistic faith fervently believed that the United States, following its destiny, would eventually annex the entire Western Hemisphere from the Arctic snows to Cape Horn. And in 1956 they came very close indeed to success in Nicaragua, when William Walker made himself president of that harassed republic, the only time in history a native-born American has become the head of another sovereign nation. If Walker had then acted with discretion the whole history of the Americans might have been changed, for he and most of the

29

other rampaging filibusters were proslavery southerners whose enthusiasm for American expansion was linked with the desire to gain new lands for that "peculiar institution."

The times favored a spirit of enthusiastic nationalism and an unshakable conviction of the superiority of the United States over all other nations. Few Americans then cared what the rest of the world thought of them—what they thought of the rest of the world was all that mattered. Even the federal government caught the fever of expansion; the Administration of President Franklin Pierce (1853–57) approached Russia about the purchase of Alaska, broached the matter of annexation with the king of the Hawaiian Islands, attempted to buy Cuba from Spain, and made overtures toward the purchase of a large naval base in the Dominican Republic. None of these efforts succeeded at the time, however, and the only tangible gain of territory was the land acquired along the Mexican border by the Gadsden Purchase of 1853.

Most of the filibusters, who sought to gain by force what their government could not acquire by diplomacy, were men of the frontier with a good leavening of Mississippi River men of the "half-horse-half-alligator" type. There was a certain proportion of barflies and drifters from the slums of the big cities, but the officers and hard core of these adventurers must have been a magnificent lot of men, the pick of the frontiersmen of the time. An English explorer wrote of some of William Walker's followers in Nicaragua: "Tall, upright, broad-shouldered men they were nearly all. Their heads were well set on, hands and feet small, muscles like iron . . . the very pick of the Western States—men highly thought of even there for reckless daring. . . . They were simply the most good-natured, good-tempered fellows I ever met with."

The filibusters used two general methods of operation. The first was a slambang landing on the coast of one of the southern republics and the proclamation of a new government with the invaders holding all the key offices. But this forthright procedure was so blatantly crude and smacked so of piracy that it outraged public opinion not only in the country attacked but throughout the world; it never gained more than the initial local success of surprise.

The more successful method was for a group of Americans to enlist as a distinct corps in one of the warring factions in the new Spanish-speaking republics. For a while these volunteers were eagerly sought by the revolutionary leaders because of their superb fighting qualities; they were recruited by promises of sizable tracts of land—the idea being that these soldiers of fortune, after victory was attained, would settle down as solid citizens to enjoy the rewards of victory. The danger, however, was that these adventurers, as a compact and disciplined body, would seize the government itself. This is exactly what William Walker and his followers accomplished in Nicaragua, in the filibuster which came nearest to permanent success.

Walker's filibustering career had begun two years before—with a fiasco. In the autumn of 1853 he had descended with forty-odd followers on lower California and proclaimed it an independent republic with himself as president. When reinforcements arrived he extended his sway on paper by a proclamation annexing the neighboring state of Sonora to his newly established nation and the San Francisco newspaper *Alta California* aptly noted, "It would have been just as cheap and easy to have annexed the whole of Mexico at once, and would have saved the trouble of making future proclamations." The whole affair was ridiculous on the surface but not so funny to some of the people immediately in Walker's way, for he had a deadly determination and never hesitated to execute anyone who obstructed his purpose. Chased out of Lower California, he managed to lead 33 surviving followers back to safety across the boarder below San Diego on May 8, 1854, which happened to be his thirtieth birthday.

But from this initial defeat Walker was to go on to become the grand master of the filibusters. One would imagine that the leader of such hard-bitten daredevils must have been a man of splendid physique and overwhelming personality. But Walker was nothing of the sort. He was about as innocuous looking as a man could be. Only about five feet, five inches in height, he weighed just over a hundred pounds. His hair and eyebrows were tow-white and his pale face was covered with the freckles which usually go with such coloring. His expression was heavy and he was taciturn to an extreme, but when he spoke he gained attention with the first word uttered. His eyes were his striking features: all noticed their piercing gray coldness and he became known as "the gray-eyed man of destiny."

Born in Nashville, Tennessee, in 1824 of Scotch-Irish ancestry, Walker had studied medicine in Europe but turned to the law in Nashville and New Orleans upon his return. Then he became a journalist and moved to California, where he edited a newspaper in San Francisco, but later he practiced law again in Maryville until in October, 1853, he sailed with 45 followers from San Francisco for his invasion of Lower California.

His first humiliating failure in that expedition taught Walker a few lessons but in no way cured him of the filibustering fever. In 1855 he was off again, this time to Nicaragua. There, instead of making a rash and forthright landing, he gained entry as the leader of a band of soldier-colonists who were to serve under the banner of the Outs (who happened to be the Liberals) in the current revolution. His followers became citizens of the country by a simple declaration of intention and were promised grants of land when their newly adopted cause won victory.

In Nicaragua Walker found a green and fertile land whose fragrant orange groves, sparkling lakes, and smoking volcanoes had so carried away an early English monk that he had called it "Mahomet's Paradise." The little country had achieved a shaky independence after the downfall of the Mexican emperor in 1823, but ever since had been kept in turmoil by civil warfare. Nicaragua had a special importance for Americans, in these years between the Gold Rush and the Golden Spike, became through it ran the favored route to California—a relatively comfortable passage from one ocean to the other by river and lake boat and a short stretch of road.

Walker's first move was to gain control of this Transit route, which would give him his vital supply line for recruits and equipment from the United States. On a sunny June morning he assembled his little army outside the Legitimist (i.e., Conservative) stronghold of Rivas, which controlled the road section of the Transit route, and about noon he led them on a reckless frontal charge into the town.

At the first shots, his native allies turned tail and left the fifty-odd Americans to fight ten times their numbers. The invaders met a steady and deadly fire as they charged toward the central plaza with wild yells and cheers (the usual head-on tactics of filibusters) and were soon forced to take shelter in several adobe houses where they were surrounded by the enemy. The Legitimists then set fire to the sheltering houses and an immediate retreat became imperative to save the survivors. The Americans sallied forth with cheers and shouts and, before the enemy could meet this unexpected offensive, pushed through the streets to the outskirts of the town. Several of the wounded were too seriously hurt to move, and these were immediately butchered by the Legitimists and their bodies burned. The enemy losses, however, were ten times those of the Americans, and thereafter no sober natives ever wanted to shoot it out at close range with the gringos.

It was a badly beaten group of survivors who re-assembled in a cacao plantation outside the town. But Walker got them safely back to their base and in August led them on another foray against the enemy force, which, though ten times as large, had consumed so much brandy to rouse their courage before the battle that the Americans won an easy victory. Walker now decided on the one really brilliant stroke of generalship in his career. The entire Legitimist army was at Rivas, leaving Grenada, the government seat, undefended. Walker loaded his entire force, now increased to 350 by recruits from the United States and native volunteers, on the Transit Line's steamer, sailed them up Lake Nicaragua and advanced at night on the unsuspecting city. They surged over an unmanned barricade and rushed at the double into the main plaza, encountering only a few scattered shots from the skeleton garrison, who then turned and fled. In a matter of hours, with the loss of one soldier, Walker was master of the enemy capital.

By his capture of Grenada, Walker put himself in a position which might very possibly have led in time to his dominance of all Central America and even, just possibly, to the eventual conquest of Cuba as well, and its consolidation into a Central American-Caribbean empire of sorts, which, based on slavery, would be a firm ally of the southern states. It was a stirring prospect and the chances are that Walker dimly glimpsed its glitter. His filings, however, were a stubborn refusal to heed the advice of experienced advisers refusal to heed the advice of experienced advisers and an overwhelming impatience, the occupational disease of almost all dictators. And these faults betrayed him.

For a while, however, he played his newly won trumps with considerable skill. First, he released about a hundred political prisoners rotting in chains and dungeons under Grenada's great cathedral. The day after the capture of the city he attended Mass at the cathedral, accompanied by many of his officers, and soon won the powerful support of the clergy by his respect for church property and traditions. Two weeks later the Legitimist commander acknowledged defeat and came into Grenada to arrange a peach. Walker put on a great show for his entry by lining the streets and the plaza with his heavily armed followers and also armed and paraded a large number of male travelers stranded in the city because of the closure of the Transit route.

The result was a treaty which ended hostilities and named Patricio Rivas, an innocuous Legitimist, temporary president of the united republic. It appointed William Walker as commander in chief of the combined armies. The Legitimist garrison at Fort San Carlos and another farther down the San Juan River then abandoned their posts, and the Transit Line was again open to free movement. Landing with 58 men, William Walker had, in effect, captured Nicaragua in a little more than four months.

But only a few months later, in February, 1856, war broke out with Nicaragua's southern neighbor, the republic of Costa Rica, which raised an army of 9,000 men and declared war on Walker's "bandits." To compound his difficulties, Walker rashly decided to seize the steamers and properties of the Transit Company. Commodore Cornelius Vanderbilt had built up this line and had given, at first, every aid and assistance to Walker, who, he hoped, would bring peace and order to the revolution-wracked country. But Walker, whose knowledge of warfare in the financial jungle was limited, chose to line up with a fact in seeking to oust Vanderbilt from control.

The old Commodore's wrath, when he heard of the confiscation, was said to have been terrible beyond description. He not only suspended the sailing of all Transit ships to Nicaragua, thus cutting Walker's supply line, but began intriguing both with the Costa Ricans and with Walker's puppet, President Rivas. Shortly after the Costa Rican army crossed the border, President Rivas went into revolt and appealed for help to the three little countries to the north—Guatemala, El Salvador, and Honduras. Walker met this crisis by assuming formal control of the government. On July 12, 1856, with a grand parade through the main square of Grenada, he took the oath of office as president of Nicaragua. The American minister to Nicaragua, John H. Wheeler, a friend of Walker's, rashly took it upon himself to recognize the new government, but when the news reached Washington, Secretary, of State Marcy recalled Wheeler and forced his resignation.

Some of Walker's proclamations, during the months between his formal accession to power and his downfall, were drastic. He confiscated many of the natives' estates to raise money, placed English on an equal legal basis with Spanish, and made changes in the land laws with the frank purpose of placing "a large portion of the land of the country in the hands of the white race"—meaning his own followers. Most potentially fateful was his decree relegalizing slavery, which had been abolished thirty years before. The significance of this decree was that Walker, rebuffed in his diplomatic overtures to the government at Washington, was casting his lot with the southern states in the impending Civil War. There is reason to believe that some of the southern leaders shared Walker's dream of a Latin American slave union as an ally in their own struggle.

None of these decrees ever went into effect because Walker's time was running out. By October he was under attack from the south by the Costa Ricans, and from the north by the combined armies of Guatemala, El Salvador, and Honduras. In this crisis Walker decided to evacuate Grenada and to move his headquarters to the volcanic island of Ometepe on Lake Nicaragua. In order to deny his enemies the prestige of a conquest, he left his second in command, Charles Frederick Henningsen, a British soldier of fortune, at Grenada with orders to destroy the city utterly.

Henningsen organized his men into demolition detachments and systematically began to blow up and burn the buildings section by section, while the hysterical natives streamed out of the city. Henningsen's men naturally found loot and wines and spirits in most of the houses they entered. Henningsen was unable to restrain his officers and they, in turn, lost all control of their men. As nightfall came, the city became an obscenity with flames shooting skyward, clouds of smoke hugging the roof tops, and groups of howling drunk, smoke-blackened filibusters screaming and reeling through the streets in an orgy of plunder and destruction. For two days and two nights this bedlam of annihilation rose to a crescendo as the crazed Americans drank and plundered, smashed and fired buildings, fell in a drunken stupor from which they would be awakened, likely as not, by the kicks of yelling and singing comrades, to rise dizzily and stagger on to smash and fire other buildings in the ranging inferno of explosions and smoke—and to drink some more.

The enemy forces presently attacked the city from three different sides and one column seized the Guadalupe church, which stood on the street running between the wharf on Lake Nicaragua and the main plaza where Henningsen was rallying his men.

After setting fire to all the surrounding buildings, he began to fight his way, foot by foot, down the street toward the wharf. At first, many of the Americans were still half drunk, and some took to the bottle again in the face of such imminent danger. Somehow Henningsen finally got them sober and into a kind of order. A filibuster named Calvin O'Neal, whose brother had fallen in the first onslaughts, came to Henningsen in a frenzy of raging grief and asked permission to charge a body of 400 or 500 Guatemalan soldiers who could be seen forming in the distance. His commander gave him 32 picked Rifles. What followed was later described by Walker:

"O'Neal, barefooted and in his shirt sleeves, leaped on his horse, and calling on his Rifles to follow, dashed into the midst of the allies as they firmed near the old church. The men, fired by the spirit of their leader, followed in the same fierce career, dealing death and destruction on the terrified foe. The allies were entirely unprepared for O'Neal's sudden, clashing charge, and they fell as heedless travellers before the blast of the simoom. The slaughter made by the thirty-two Rifles was fearful, and so far were O'Neal and his men carried by the 'rapture of the strife' that it was difficult for Henningsen to recall them to the Plaza. When they did return it was through streets almost blocked with the bodies of the Guatemalans they had slain."

By the next morning Henningsen had concentrated his forces in the main plaza and could count his strength. He had lost 23 men killed or captured and could muster only 227 soldiers fit for duty; he was burdened with 73 wounded and some 70 women and children and sick.

Two days later, on November 27, after blowing up a church on the plaza and destroying the nearby buildings (Henningsen was still carrying out his orders amidst the inferno), he poured a heavy artillery fire into the Guadalupe church and captured it by an immediately following assault by 60 picked Rifles. At once he moved all his forces and supplies into this large, strong building and prepared to withstand a siege until Walker could relieve him from the lake. His men had recovered from their debauchery and were willing to work and fight for their lives and for the protection of all the noncombatants. But the crowded and unsanitary conditions in the church, the food of mule and horse meat, the night chills and rains, and the stench from the unburied enemy dead outside brought much sickness to the 400 Americans huddled together, and cholera soon appeared as a far more dreadful foe than the enemy.

A ministering angel appeared amidst these terrible scenes, Mrs. Edward Bingham, the wife of an invalid actor who had brought his family to Nicaragua to take up one of Walker's grants of land to American settlers. From the time of her arrival she had nursed in the American hospitals, and in the Guadalupe church she constantly tended the sick and wounded with magnificent courage and complete self-sacrifice which gained her the deepest gratitude of all the soldiers. Finally, worn out and weak, she became another victim of the dreaded cholera and died within a few hours. Her children perished with her, but her invalid husband survived all the horrors of the siege and eventually reached California safely. Of all the Americans in Nicaragua this splendid woman showed the finest spirit.

For two harrowing weeks Henningsen held out while Walker stood off Grenada in the lake steamer *Virgen,* watching for a chance to extricate Henningsen's forces. Then, during the first week in December, 300 recruits arrived from New Orleans and San Francisco, well-equipped men in fine fettle and spoiling for a fight. Of these, 160 were organized as a relief force and placed under the command of the cavalry leader, Colonel John Waters. Waters landed his men and silently led them toward the city. By dawn he had stormed over all the enemy barricades and had joined Henningsen, with a loss of about a fourth of his men. The Americans, who had been slowly extending their lines from the Guadalupe church down the street toward the water, quickly seized the wharf and embarked the survivors on the *Virgen* without enemy opposition.

General Henningsen, before he boarded the rescuing steamer, cast one last look back at the ruined city. Then he thrust a lance into the ground and to it attached a piece of rawhide upon which he had written, *Aqui fué Grenada*—"Here was Grenada."

Walker was not licked yet. He still commanded 900 men and controlled the Transit route, over which he expected several hundred reinforcements. But his enemies included, along with four sovereign states, the redoubtable Commodore Vanderbilt. Early in the autumn of 1856 the Commodore had dispatched to Costa Rica a young secret agent named Sylvanus Spencer with a well-planned scheme to seize the Transit route and bottle up the filibusters. With a small Costa Rican force and a boldness worthy of Walker himself, Spencer swooped down on one of Walker's garrisons, seized the river steamers, and cut off the filibuster reinforcements. By April, 1857, Walker's force was trapped at Rivas, with no hope of escape. By arrangement with the Central American armies he surrendered to an American naval officer, Commander Charles H. Davis, and was spirited off to New Orleans, where he received a hero's welcome.

Three more times William Walker and his followers attempted to invade Nicaragua without success. On the last attempt Walker surrendered to a British naval officer, who turned him over to the Honduran authorities, from whom he received short shrift. On September 12, 1860, he met his death before an adobe wall at the hands of a firing squad, an end which he had decreed so often for his political enemies. He was buried in an unmarked grave which Joaquin Miller commemorated in his poem "That Night in Nicaragua." Despite his ruthlessness and unappealing personality, Walker held the constant loyalty of many of his followers through all his later failures and, surprisingly enough, that of many of the natives as well. His men were beyond description daring. His able lieutenant, General Henningsen, years later wrote a fitting epitaph for these Homeric men of Nicaragua:

"I was on the Confederate side in many of the bloodiest battles of the late war; but I aver that if, at the end of that war, I had been allowed to pick five thousand of the bravest Confederate or Federal soldiers I ever saw, and could resurrect and pit against them one thousand or such men as lie beneath the orange trees of Nicaragua, I feel certain that the thousand would have scattered and utterly routed the five thousand within an hour. All military science failed, on a suddenly given field, before assailants who came on at run, to close with their revolvers, and who thought little of charging a battery, pistol in hand. . . .

"Such men do not turn of in the average of everyday life, nor do I ever expect to see their like again."

The New View
of Reconstruction

Eric Foner

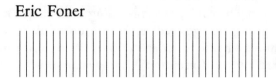

In the past twenty years, no period of American history has been the subject of a more thoroughgoing reevaluation than Reconstruction—the violent, dramatic, and still controversial era following the Civil War. Race relations, politics, social life, and economic change during Reconstruction have all been reinterpreted in the light of changed attitudes toward the place of blacks within American society. If historians have not yet forged a fully satisfying portrait of Reconstruction as a whole, the traditional interpretation that dominated historical writing for much of this century has irrevocably been laid to rest.

Anyone who attended high school before 1960 learned that Reconstruction was an era of unrelieved sordidness in American political and social life. The martyred Lincoln, according to this view, had planned a quick and painless readmission of the Southern states as equal members of the national family. President Andrew Johnson, his successor, attempted to carry out Lincoln's policies but was foiled by the Radical Republicans (also known as Vindictives or Jacobins). Motivated by an irrational hatred of Rebels or by ties with Northern capitalists out to plunder the South, the Radicals swept aside Johnson's lenient program and fastened black supremacy upon the defeated Confederacy. An orgy of corruption followed, presided over by unscrupulous carpet-baggers (Northerners who ventured south to reap the spoils of office), traitorous scalawags (Southern whites who cooperated with the new governments for personal gain), and the ignorant and childlike freemen, who were incapable of properly exercising the political power that had been thrust upon them. After much needless suffering, the white community of

37

the South banded together to overthrow these "black" governments and restore home rule (their euphemism for white supremacy). All told, Reconstruction was just about the darkest page in American saga.

Originating in anti-Reconstruction propaganda of Southern Democrats during the 1870s, this traditional interpretation achieved scholarly legitimacy around the turn of the century through the work of William Dunning and his students at Columbia University. It reached the larger pubic through films like *Birth of a Nation* and *Gone With the Wind* and that best-selling work of myth-making masquerading as history, *The Tragic Era* by Claude G. Bowers. In language as exaggerated as it was colorful, Bowers told how Andrew Johnson "fought the bravest battle for constitutional liberty and for the preservation of our institutions ever waged by an Executive" but was overwhelmed by the "poisonous propaganda" of the Radicals. Southern whites, as a result, "literally were put to the torture" by "emissaries of hate" who manipulated the "simple-minded" freedmen, "inflaming the negroes' egotism" and even inspiring "lustful assaults" by blacks upon white womanhood.

In a discipline that sometimes seems to pride itself on the rapid rise and fall of historical interpretations, this traditional portrait of Reconstruction enjoyed remarkable staying power. The long reign of the old interpretation is not difficult to explain. It presented a set of easily identifiable heroes and villains. It enjoyed the imprimatur of the nation's leading scholars. And it accorded with the political and social realties of the first half of this century. This image of Reconstruction helped freeze the mind of the white South in unalterable opposition to any movement for breaching the ascendancy of the Democratic party, eliminating segregation, or readmitting disfranchised blacks to the vote.

Nevertheless, the demise of the traditional interpretation was inevitable, for it ignored the testimony of the central participant in the drama of Reconstruction—the black freedman. Furthermore, it was grounded in the conviction that blacks were unfit to share in political power. As Dunning's Columbia colleague John W. Burgess put it, "A black skin means membership in a race of men which has never of itself succeeded in subjecting passion to reason, has never, therefore, created any civilization of any kind." Once objective scholarship and modern experience rendered that assumption untenable, the entire edifice was bound to fall.

The work of "revising" the history of Reconstruction began with the writings of a handful of survivors of the era, such as John A. Lynch, who had served as a black congressman from Mississippi after the Civil War. In the 1930s white scholars like Francis Simkins and Robert Woody carried the task forward. Then, in 1935, the black historian and activist W.E.B. Du Bois produced *Black Reconstruction in America*, a monumental reevaluation that closed with an irrefutable indictment of a historical profession that had sacrificed scholarly objectivity on the altar of racial bias. "One fact and one alone," he wrote, "explains the attitude of most recent writers toward Reconstruction; they cannot conceive of Negroes as men." Du Bois's work, however, was ignored by most historians.

It was not until the 1960s that the full force of the revisionist wave broke over the field. Then, in rapid succession, virtually every assumption of the traditional viewpoint was systematically dismantled. A drastically different portrait emerged to take its place. President Lincoln did not have a coherent "plan" for Reconstruction, but at the time of his assassination he had been cautiously contemplating black suffrage. Andrew Johnson was a stubborn, racist politician who lacked the ability to compromise. By isolating himself from the broad currents of public opinion that had nourished Lincoln's career, Johnson created an impasse with Congress that Lincoln would certainly have avoided, thus throwing away his political power and destroying his own plans for reconstructing the South.

The Radicals in Congress were acquitted of both vindictive motives and the charge of serving as the stalking-horses of Northern capitalism. They emerged instead as idealists in the best nineteenth-century reform tradition. Radical leaders like Charles Sumner and Thaddeus Stevens had worked for the rights of blacks long before any conceivable political advantage flowed from such a commitment. Stevens refused to sign the Pennsylvania Constitution of 1838 because it disfranchised the state's black citizens; Sumner led a fight in the 1850s to integrate Boston's public schools. Their Reconstruction policies were based on principle, not petty political advantage, for the central issue dividing Johnson and these Radical Republicans was the civil rights of freedmen. Studies of congressional policy-making, such as Eric L. McKitrick's *Andrew Johnson and Reconstruction*, also revealed that Reconstruction legislation, ranging from the Civil Rights Act of 1866 to the Fourteenth and Fifteenth Amendments, enjoyed broad support from moderate and conservative Republicans. It was not simply the work of a narrow radical faction.

Even more startling was the revised portrait of Reconstruction in the South itself. Imbued with the spirit of the civil rights movement and rejecting entirely the racial assumptions that had underpinned the traditional interpretation, these historians evaluated Reconstruction from the black point of view. Works like Joel Williamson's *After Slavery* portrayed the period as a time of extraordinary political, social, and economic progress for blacks. The establishment of public school systems, the granting of equal citizenship to blacks, the effort to restore the devastated Southern economy, the attempt to construct an interracial political democracy from the ashes of slavery, all these were commendable achievements, not the elements of Bower's "tragic era."

Unlike earlier writers, the revisionists stressed the active role of the freedmen in shaping Reconstruction. Black initiative established as many schools as did Northern religious societies and the Freedmen's Bureau. The right to vote was not simply thrust upon them by meddling outsiders, since blacks began agitating for the suffrage as soon as they were freed. In 1865 black conventions throughout the south issued eloquent, though unheeded, appeals for equal civil and political rights.

With the advent of Radical Reconstruction in 1867, the freedmen did enjoy a real measure of political power. But black supremacy never existed. In most states blacks held only a small fraction of political offices, and even in South Carolina, where they comprised a majority of the state legislature's lower house, effective power remained in white hands.

As for corruption, moral standards in both government and private enterprise were at low ebb throughout the nation in the postwar years—the era of Boss Tweed, the Credit Mobilier scandal, and the Whiskey Ring. Southern corruption could hardly be blamed on former slaves.

Other actors in the Reconstruction drama also came in for reevaluation. Most carpetbaggers were former Union soldiers seeking economic opportunity in the postwar South, not unscrupulous adventures. Their motives, a typically American amalgam of humanitarianism and the pursuit of profit, were no more insidious than those of Western pioneers. Scalawags, previously seen as traitors to the white race, now emerged as "Old Line" Whig Unionists who had opposed secession in the first place or as poor whites who had long resented planters' domination of Southern life and who saw in Reconstruction a chance to recast Southern society along more democratic lines. Strongholds of Southern white Republicanism like east Tennessee and western North Carolina had been the scene of resistance to Confederate rule throughout the Civil War; now, as one scalawag newspaper put it, the choice was "between salvation at the hand of the Negro or destruction at the hand of the rebels."

At the same time, the Ku Klux Klan and kindred groups, whose campaign of violence against black and white Republicans had been minimized or excused in older writings, were portrayed as they really were. Earlier scholars had conveyed the impression that the Klan intimidated blacks mainly by dressing as ghosts and playing on the freedmen's superstitions. In fact, black fears were all too real: the Klan was a terrorist organization that beat and killed its political opponents to deprive blacks of their newly won rights. The complicity of the Democratic party and the silence of prominent whites in the face of such outrages stood as an indictment of the moral code the South had inherited from the days of slavery.

By the end of the 1960s, then, the old interpretation had been completely reversed. Southern freedmen were the heroes, the "Redeemers" who overthrew Reconstruction were the villains, and if the era was "tragic," it was because change did not go far enough. Reconstruction had been a time of real progress and its failure a lost opportunity for the South and the nation. But the legacy of Reconstruction—the Fourteenth and Fifteenth Amendments—endured to inspire future efforts for civil rights. As Kenneth Stampp wrote in *The Era of Reconstruction*, a superb summary of revisionist findings published in 1965, "If it was worth four years of civil war to save the Union, it was worth a few years of radical reconstruction to give the American Negro the ultimate promise of equal civil and political rights."

As Stampp's statement suggests, the reevaluation of the first Reconstruction was inspired in large measure by the impact of the second—the modern civil rights movement. And with the waning of that movement in recent years, writing on Reconstruction has undergone still another transformation. Instead of seeing the Civil War and its aftermath as a second American Revolution (as Charles Beard had), a regression into barbarism (as Bowers argued), or a golden opportunity squandered (as the revisionists saw it), recent writers argue that Radical Reconstruction was not really very radical. Since land was not distributed to the former slaves, they remained economically dependent upon their former owners. The planter class survived both the war and Reconstruction with its property (apart from slaves) and prestige more or less intact.

Not only changing times but also the changing concerns of historians have contributed to this latest reassessment of Reconstruction. The hallmark of the past decade's historical writing has been an emphasis upon "social history"—the evocation of the past lives of ordinary Americans—and the downplaying of strictly political events. When applied to Reconstruction, this concern with the "social" suggested that black suffrage and officeholding, once seen as the most radical departures of the Reconstruction era, were relatively insignificant.

Recent historians have focused their investigations not upon the politics of Reconstruction but upon the social and economic aspects of the transition from slavery to freedom. Herbert Gutman's influential study of the black family during and after slavery found little change in family structure or relations between men and women resulting from emancipation. Under slavery most blacks had lived in nuclear family units, although they faced the constant threat of separation from loved ones by sale. Reconstruction provided the opportunity for blacks to solidify their preexisting family ties. Conflicts over whether black women should work in the cotton fields (planters said yes, many black families said no) and over white attempts to "apprentice" black children revealed that the autonomy of family life was a major preoccupation of the freedmen. Indeed, whether manifested in their withdrawal from churches controlled by whites, in the blossoming of black fraternal, benevolent, and self-improvement organizations, or in the demise of the slave quarters and their replacement by small tenant farms occupied by individual families, the quest for independence from white authority and control over their own day-to-day lives shaped the black response to emancipation.

In the post-Civil War South the surest guarantee of economic autonomy, blacks believed, was land. To the freedmen the justice of a claim to land based on their years of unrequited labor appeared self-evident. As an Alabama black convention put it, "The property which they [the planters] hold was nearly all earned by the sweat of *our* brows." As Leon Litwack showed in *Been in the Storm So Long*, a Pulitzer Prize-winning account of the black response to emancipation, many freedmen in 1865 and 1866 refused to sign labor contracts, expecting the federal government to give them land. In some localities, as one Alabama overseer reported, they "set up claims to the plantation and all on it."

In the end, of course, the vast majority of Southern blacks remained propertyless and poor. But exactly why the South, and especially its black population, suffered from dire poverty and economic retardation in the decades following the Civil War is a matter of much dispute. In *One Kind of Freedom*, economists Roger Ransom and Richard Sutch indicted country merchants for monopolizing credit and charging usurious interest rates, forcing black tenants into debt and locking the South into a dependence on cotton production that impoverished the entire region. But Jonathan Wiener, in his study of postwar Alabama, argued that planters used their political power to compel blacks to remain on the plantations. Planters succeeded in stabilizing the plantation system, but only by blocking the growth of alternative enterprises, like factories, that might draw off black laborers, thus locking the region into a pattern of economic backwardness.

If the thrust of recent writing has emphasized the social and economic aspects of Reconstruction, politics has not been entirely neglected. But political studies have also reflected the postrevisionist mood summarized by C. Vann Woodward when he observed "how essentially nonrevolutionary and conservative Reconstruction really was." Recent writers, unlike their revisionist predecessors, have found little to praise in federal policy toward the emancipated blacks.

A new sensitivity to the strength of prejudice and laissez-faire ideas in the nineteenth-century North has led many historians to doubt whether the Republican party ever made a genuine commitment to racial justice in the South. The granting of black suffrage was an alternative to a long-term federal responsibility for protecting the rights of the former slaves. Once enfranchised, blacks could be left to fend for themselves. With the exception of a few Radicals like Thaddeus Stevens, nearly all Northern policy-makers and educators are criticized today for assuming that, so long as the unfettered operations of the marketplace afforded blacks the opportunity to advance through diligent labor, federal efforts to assist them in acquiring land were unnecessary.

Probably the most innovative recent writing on Reconstruction politics has centered on a broad reassessment of black Republicanism, largely undertaken by a new generation of black historians. Scholars like Thomas Holt and Nell Painter insist that Reconstruction was not simply a matter of black and white. Conflicts within the black community, no less than divisions among whites, shaped Reconstruction politics. Where revisionist scholars, both black and white, had celebrated the accomplishments of black political leaders, Holt, Painter, and others charge that they failed to address the economic plight of the black masses. Painter criticized "representative colored men," as national black leaders were called, for failing to provide ordinary freedmen with effective political leadership. Holt found that black office-holders in South Carolina mostly emerged from the old free mulatto class of Charleston, which shared many assumptions with prominent whites. "Basically bourgeois in their origins and orientation," he wrote, they "failed to act in the interest of black peasants."

In emphasizing the persistence from slavery of divisions between free blacks and slaves, these writers reflect the increasing concern with continuity and conservatism in Reconstruction. Their work reflects a startling extension of revisionist premises. If, as has been argued for the past twenty years, blacks were active agents rather than mere victims of manipulation, then they could not be absolved of blame for the ultimate failure of Reconstruction.

Despite the excellence of recent writing and the continual expansion of our knowledge of the period, historians of Reconstruction today face a unique dilemma. An old interpretation has been overthrown, but a coherent new synthesis has yet to take its place. The revisionists of the 1960s effectively established a series of negative points: the

Reconstruction governments were not as bad as had been portrayed, black supremacy was a myth, the Radicals were not cynical manipulators of the freedmen. Yet no convincing over-all portrait of the quality of political and social life emerged from their writings. More recent historians have rightly pointed to elements of continuity that spanned the nineteenth-century Southern experience, especially the survival, in modified form, of the plantation system. Nevertheless, by denying the real changes that did occur, they have failed to provide a convincing portrait of an era characterized above all by drama, turmoil, and so-cial change.

Building upon the findings of the past twenty years of scholarship, a new portrait of Reconstruction ought to begin by viewing it not as a specific time period, bounded by the years 1865 and 1877, but as an episode in a prolonged historical process—American society's adjustment to the consequences of the Civil War and emancipation. The Civil War, of course, raised the decisive questions of America's national existence: the relations between local and national authority, the definition of citizenship, the balance between force and consent in generating obedience to authority. The war and Reconstruction, as Allan Nevins observed over fifty years ago, marked the ''emergence of modern America.'' This was the era of the completion of the national railroad network, the creation of the modern steel industry, the conquest of the West and final subduing of the Indians, and the expansion of the mining frontier. Lincoln's America—the world of the small farm and ar-tisan shop—gave way to a rapidly industrializing economy. The issues that galvanized postwar Northern politics—from the question of the greenback currency to the mode of paying holders of the national debt—arose from the economic changes unleashed by the Civil War.

Above all, the war irrevocably abolished slavery. Since 1619, when ''twenty negars'' disembarked from a Dutch ship in Virginia, racial injustice had haunted American life, mocking its professed ideals even as tobacco and cotton, the products of slave labor, helped finance the nation's economic development. Now the implications of the black presence could no longer be ignored. The Civil War resolved the problem of slavery but, as the Philadelphia diarist Sydney George Fisher observed in June 1865, it opened an even more intractable problem: ''What shall we do with the Negro?'' Indeed, he went on, this was a problem ''*incapable* of any solution that will satisfy both North and South.''

As Fisher realized, the focal point of Reconstruction was the social revolution known as emancipation. Plantation slavery was simultaneously a system of labor, a form of racial domination, and the foundation upon which arose a distinctive ruling class within the South. Its demise threw open the most fundamental questions of economy, society, and politics. A new system of labor, social, racial, and political relations had to be created to replace slavery.

The United States was not the only nation to experience emancipation in the nine-teenth century. Neither plantation slavery nor abolition were unique to the United States. But Reconstruction was. In a comparative perspective Radical Reconstruction stands as a remarkable experiment, the only effort of a society experiencing abolition to bring the former slaves within the umbrella of equal citizenship. Because the Radicals did not achieve everything they wanted, historians have lately tended to play down the stunning departure represented by black suffrage and officeholding. Former slaves, most fewer than two years removed from bondage, debated the fundamental questions of the polity: What is a republican form of government? Should the state provide equal education for all? How could political equality be reconciled with a society in which property was so unequally distributed? There was something inspiring in the way such men met the challenge of Reconstruction. "I knew nothing more than to obey my master," James K. Greene, an Alabama black politician later recalled. "But the tocsin of freedom sounded and knocked at the door and we walked out like free men and we met the exigencies as they grew up, and shouldered the responsibilities."

"You never saw a people more excited on the subject of politics than are the negroes of the south," one planter observed in 1867. And there were more than a few Southern whites as well who in these years shook off the prejudices of the past to embrace the vision of a new South dedicated to the principles of equal citizenship and social justice. One ordinary South Carolinian expressed the new sense of possibility in 1868 to the Republican governor of the state: "I am sorry that I cannot write an elegant stiled letter to your excellency. But I rejoice to think that God almighty has given to the poor of S.C. a Gov. to hear to feel to protect the humble poor without distinction to race or color. . . . I am a native borned S. C. a poor man never owned a Negro in my life nor my father before me. . . . Remember the true and loyal are the poor of the whites and blacks, outside of these you can find none loyal."

Few modern scholars believe the Reconstruction governments established in the South in 1867 and 1868 fulfilled the aspirations of their humble constituents. While their achievements in such realms as education, civil rights, and the economic rebuilding of the South are now widely appreciated, historians today believe they failed to affect either the economic plight of the emancipated slave or the ongoing transformation of independent white farmers into cotton tenants. Yet their opponents did perceive the Reconstruction governments in precisely this way—as representatives of a revolution that had put the bottom rail, both racial and economic, on top. This perception helps explain the ferocity of the attacks leveled against them and the pervasiveness of violence in the postemancipation South.

The spectacle of black men voting and holding office was anathema to large numbers of Southern whites. Even more disturbing, at least in the view of those who still controlled the plantation regions of the South, was the emergence of local officials, black and white, who sympathized with the plight of the black laborer. Alabama's vagrancy law was a "dead letter" in 1870, "because those who are charged with its enforcement are indebted to the vagrant vote for their offices and emoluments." Political debates over the level and incidence of taxation, the control of crops, and the resolution of contract disputes revealed that a primary issue of Reconstruction was the role of government in a plantation society. During presidential Reconstruction, and after "Redemption," with planters and their allies in control of politics, the law emerged as a means of stabilizing and promoting the plantation system. If Radical Reconstruction failed to redistribute the land of the South, the ouster of the planter class from control of politics at least ensured that the sanctions of the criminal law would not be employed to discipline the black labor force.

An understanding of this fundamental conflict over the relation between government and society helps explain the pervasive complaints concerning corruption and "extravagance" during the Radical Reconstruction. Corruption there was aplenty; tax rates did rise sharply. More significant than the rate of taxation, however, was the change in its incidence. For the first time, planters and white farmers had to pay a significant portion of their income to the government, while propertyless blacks often escaped scot-free. Several states, moreover, enacted heavy taxes on uncultivated land to discourage land speculation and force land onto the market, benefiting, it was hoped, the freedmen.

As time passed, complaints about the "extravagance" and corruption of Southern governments found a sympathetic audience among influential Northerners. The Democratic charge that universal suffrage in the South was responsible for high taxes and governmental extravagance coincided with a rising conviction among the urban middle classes of the North that city government had to be taken out of the hands of the immigrant poor and returned to the "best men"—the educated, professional, financially independent citizens unable to exert much political influence at a time of mass parties and machine politics. Increasingly the "respectable" middle classes began to retreat from the very notion of universal suffrage. The poor were no longer perceived as honest producers, the backbone of the social order; now they became the "dangerous classes," the "mob." As the historian Francis Parkman put it, too much power rested with "masses of imported ignorance and hereditary ineptitude." To Parkman the Irish of the Northern cities and the blacks of the South were equally incapable of utilizing the ballot: "Witness the municipal corruptions of New York, and the monstrosities of negro rule in South Carolina." Such attitudes helped to justify Northern inaction as, one by one, the Reconstruction regimes of the South were overthrown by political violence.

In the end, then, neither the abolition of slavery nor Reconstruction succeeded in resolving the debate over the meaning of freedom in American life. Twenty years before the American Civil War, writing about the prospect of abolition in France's colonies, Alexis de Tocqueville had written, "If the Negroes have the right to become free, the [planters] have the incontestable right not to be ruined by the Negroes' freedom." And in the United States, as in nearly every plantation society that experienced the end of slavery, a rigid social and political dichotomy between former master and former slave, an ideology of racism, and a dependent labor force with limited economic opportunities all survived abolition. Unless one means by freedom the simple fact of not being a slave, emancipation thrust blacks into a kind of no-man's land, a partial freedom that made a mockery of the American ideal of equal citizenship.

Yet by the same token the ultimate outcome underscores the uniqueness of Reconstruction itself. Alone among the societies that abolished slavery in the nineteenth century, the United States, for a moment, offered the freedmen a measure of political control over their own destinies. However brief its sway, Reconstruction allowed a scope for a remarkable political and social mobilization of the black community. It opened doors of opportunity that could never be completely closed. Reconstruction transformed the lives of Southern blacks in ways unmeasurable by statistics and unreachable by law. It raised their expectations and aspirations, redefined their status in relation to the larger society, and allowed space for the creation of institutions that enabled them to survive the repression that followed. And it established constitutional principles of civil and political equality that, while flagrantly violated after Redemption, planted the seeds of future struggle.

Certainly, in terms of the sense of possibility with which it opened, Reconstruction failed. But as Du Bois observed, it was a "splendid failure." For its animating vision—a society in which social advancement would be open to all on the basis of individual merit, not inherited caste distinctions—is as old as America itself and remains relevant to a nation still grappling with the unresolved legacy of emancipation.

They Didn't Know What Time It Was

William Peirce Randel

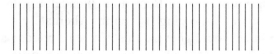

Throughout most of the last century, very few Americans could agree on the time of day. Every town kept its own time of day. Every town kept its own time. A pocket diary for the year 1873 contains two tables, one showing the difference in time between Boston and other cities, the second giving the time in other cities, the second giving the time in other cities when it was noon in New York. With a little calculating, a Boston salesman bound for St. Louis could learn from the first table that if he set his watch back one hour, sixteen minutes, and forty-six seconds, it would agree with the time-pieces of his prospective customers. And a New Yorker bound for Bangor, Maine, would be late for appointments if he forgot to set his watch *ahead* by twenty-one minutes.

There were thirty-eight different times in Wisconsin; there were six in Pittsburgh.

Great Britain had taken care of a similar situation by standardizing its time in 1848, and most of Western Europe had followed suit. But Americans could not seen to agree on a solution to the absurd problem.

For most of human history it hadn't been a problem at all. Through the centuries local time was based on noon as the moment when the sun was observed to be, at any given place on earth, directly overhead. Astronomers had long known that, thanks to the Earth's titled axis, that moment differed by as much as half an hour during the course of the year. Reliance on sundials, accordingly, produced mornings and afternoons of varying length, but that mattered little until the thirteenth century, when clocks were introduced in Europe. Their unvarying mechanism forced the invention of mean solar time, a mathematical averaging of the sun's annual vagaries. Welcome advance though this was, it did nothing to reduce the confusion caused by the variety of local times from east to west. Only the arbitrary imposition of a uniform time for an entire nation could solve the confusion.

Geography does much to explain the delay in the United States. In relatively small Western European nations the shift from local to national time was nowhere as much as half an hour. But the United States, spanning a continent, extended sixty degrees, representing four hours of the sun's daily advance. A single uniform time for so great a distance would mean that when it was noon in Boston or Philadelphia, the sun over San Francisco would be three hours short of reaching its zenith. Alternately, a base meridian located in the middle of the continent would give the East Coast its midday an hour and a half late.

Before 1800 few Americans had any need or desire to travel far from their farm or village homes, but the decades preceding the Civil War industrialization increased mobility and with it dissatisfaction with the multiplicity of local times. By the 1870s American business was finding this multiplicity more and more troublesome.

New England, smallest of the nation's regions and the most heavily industrialized, pioneered in the reduction of local times. By the early 1870s the urban areas near the Atlantic Ocean, agreed to accept Boston time, as provided by astronomers at Harvard, while the western half of the region followed Yale in adopting New York time. In most parts of the country, however, the greater distances between cities discouraged such cooperation.

Morse's telegraph, considerably improved since its first demonstration in 1844, enabled observatories to transmit electric time signals to any city willing to pay for the service. The signal was usually sent on the stroke of noon where the observatory was located, and the recipient was almost always a prominent jeweler. The clock in his shop window gave passersby a chance to check their watches, and he usually had the further responsibility of keeping the municipal clocks synchronized. In a few Eastern cities time balls dropping at noon upon direct signal from observatories offered widely visible means for correcting individual timepieces. As in England, where every harbor of any importance had a time ball, the original purpose was to aid navigation. The device has long been superseded, of course, but one time ball does survive, watched at midnight instead of at noon by huge crowds in Times Square on New Year's Eve. There were also time-guns, activated by the same telegraphed signals, for the benefit of fogbound mariners.

As early as 1856 the Dudley Observatory in Albany offered to telegraph the exact time to any two clocks in New York that the city might designate. The only cost would be the original one, about seven thousand dollars, for stringing the necessary wires down the Hudson River valley. *The New York Times* applauded the offer as very liberal, adding that "the utility of a standard of time is too obvious to require argument." But the Common Council declined the offer, perhaps aware that Professor Bull of New York University had a proposal of his own. The next winter, in any event, the mayor ordered the bell ringers in all the city's fire stations to sound nine o'clock each evening upon telegraphed signal from Bull at a private observatory on Eleventh Street. "Of course," the *Times* commented, "for a night or two people will suppose the whole city is on fire at 9 o'clock. But with the hydrants frozen, the mistaken alarm will do no harm.''

In a few years the Naval Observatory in Washington became the chief source of time signals, while Western Union was gained a monopoly on their transmission. In 1877 the company installed a time ball atop its tall new building in New York. Made of copper, perforated to minimize air resistance, the three-and-a-half-foot globe poised 250 feet above street level was clearly visible throughout the harbor and business district of lower Manhattan. A *Times* editor remarked approvingly, ''In these days of railroads and railroad-like ways of doing business, a man whose time is money to him must attend not only to his hours and minutes, but even to his seconds.''

Unfortunately this second-conscious man would have been dissatisfied with the Western Union time ball; it did not always fall at exactly the right moment. The cause perhaps lay with the mechanism that had to adjust the difference in mean solar time between New York and Washington—12 minutes, 10.47 seconds. Whatever the reasons, people were calling for a system that would eliminate time differentials between major cities.

In 1882 the American Meteorological Society offered a ''Proposed Schedule for Standards of Time.'' The author leaned heavily on Harvard's eminent mathematician, Benjamin pierce, who had suggested dividing North America into time zones, each of fifteen degrees of longitude and so bounded that the differential between local sun time and the uniform zone time would nowhere be greater than thirty minutes.

Newspapers publicized the idea; readers immediately got worried. Should the entire East Coast, the asked, be forced to accept the time of some one city—Washington perhaps? Or New York? Or even Pittsburgh, as some of its local boosters insisted? People bridled particularly at Peirce's proposal to synchronize the time in all the zones with that of the Royal Naval Observatory at Greenwich, England; not even in Europe was Greenwich longitude acknowledged as the zero meridian.

If the scientific community and the newspapers hoped to prod Congress into action, they were disappointed. It would have been political suicide to ignore the strong grassroots opposition to giving up local time, which many insisted on calling ''God's Time.'' Congress did, however, adopt a resolution in 1882 calling for an international conference to choose a prime meridian for the entire world. Before this could be organized, however, the nation's railroads, of all businesses the most adversely affected by the multiplicity of local times, deciding they could wait no longer and took action of their own.

Ten years earlier, at their annual convention, railroad managers had listened politely to Charles F. Dowd, principal of a seminary for young ladies in Saratoga Springs, New York, as he outlined a plan for time zones that anticipated Peirce's. They listened to Down again in 1873, with greater interest, but the depression that year persuaded them to shelve the idea. Dowd carried his campaign to executives of other kinds of business and won considerable support. But no other enterprise had as much at stake as the railroads—or such potential influence.

Once prosperity returned, the railroad men asked one of their own, William F. Allen, to study the matter and prepare a report. As editor of the mighty *Official Guide of the Rail-*

ways and Steam Navigation Lines and as secretary of the National Railway Time Convention, Allen could speak the language of the railroad establishment as Dowd, an outsider, could not. The 1883 convention accepted his report with enthusiasm.

Announced in October 1883, the railroad plan was to take effect a month later. Public response was varied. Boston, after a town meeting dominated by university scientists, agreed to accept the railroads' Eastern time. In New York there was not even a public meeting; the mayor simply ordered all city clocks to conform, and the private sector promptly fell into line. But in Chicago things were different. The Illinois Central Railroad chose to defer the change to Central standard until the city fathers accepted it, and that, for the moment, was out of the question. A number of local working people feared that the change, of about nine minutes, might somehow result in longer working hours. But the Chicago Board of Trade and several prominent jewelers did convert, which only compounded the confusion. Meanwhile, in Washington, the superintendent of the Naval Observatory flouted the attourney general's firm opinion that no change was permissible without formal congressional approval and announced his intention to telegraph the new railroad time to all government time balls and time guns. For some years thereafter, government clocks in the District of Columbia remained on the old local time while all others showed the railroads' Eastern standard time.

For all its eventual significance for the nation's way of life, the day of the actual change—November 18, 1883, a Sunday—passed with little incident. In communities rejected the railroad plan, only clocks in railroad stations were set ahead or back. Elsewhere the curious gathered in front of jewelers' shops and then moved on, disappointed that the controversial change involved nothing more than stopping a clock for a few minutes. In New York a reporter picked up this dialogue:

"Begorra, the thing has stopped; phwahts the matter wid it, anyhow? I don't see no time changing, do you, Mike?"

"Divil a change at all, at all, can I see."

"Lave us go on, the hull thing's a sell."

"Howld your whist, will you."

"She's movin agin. Watch it now."

In a Massachusetts courtroom a few days later, a magistrate opposed to the time change found a man named Clapp in default to one Jenkins for appearing at 10:01 A.M. by the old time, which was 9:45 by the new time. When Clapp, who was to appear between 9:00 and 10:00, appealed to Superior Court, Jenkins's attorney argued that the new time was not valid because the legislature had not approved it. But the presiding judge, Oliver Wendell Holmes, Jr., ruled that Clapp had a right to be governed by the new standard.

In synchronizing time in all the zones with that of Greenwich, the railroad managers ran a certain risk, for the Prime Meridian Conference, held in Washington in the fall of 1884, might have chosen some other base for global time. the French delegates, of course, strongly opposed Greenwich, arguing instead for a meridian that passed through no major land mass—somewhere, perhaps, in the Pacific Ocean. Their logic impressed a few Americans. One wrote to an editor urging a mid-Atlantic location, and a group of

Washington clergymen plumped for the line passing through Bethlehem. But the conference concluded, by an overwhelming vote, to locate the prime meridian at Greenwich, and America's railroaders could breathe more easily.

Year by year thereafter, resistance to the railroad standard time gradually lessened, until most of the population took it for granted and called it simply standard time. But now and then the issue flared up in unexpected places. In Bath, Maine, the 1887 town meeting voted 605 to 157 to return to local time, in defiance of the state legislature. But the town officers overruled the voters and directed the mayor to keep the public clocks, at least, on standard time. He proved a veritable Solomon: the town bell would be rung, he ordered, twenty minutes early—at 6:40 and 11:40 each morning and at 12:40 and 5:40 in the afternoon, which were 7:00, noon, 1:00, and 6:00 by local time.

A year later in Georgia, Augusta rejected standard time. As reported in a local newspaper, "Without ceremony of any kind the hands of the city clock were pushed forward 32 minutes at noon, and Augusta was again placed abreast of the sun. . . . She has placed herself back alongside of old Sol's chariot now, and it is confidently believed that before many more heats have been run she will be throwing dust in his face."

Early in 1889 the Board of Education in Bellaire, Ohio, moved in the opposite direction, replacing local time with Eastern standard. Having responsibility for the municipal clock, the board could do so, and it took the opponents almost a year to nullify the monstrous action—by a city council edict making it "a misdemeanor for anyone to expose a timepiece in public with the hands marking any other than local time." When the board ignored the ordinance, all its members were arrested.

Such results were possible only when the government had not seen fit to make standard time official. A bill with that intention was submitted in 1889, but its sponsor, named Flowers, found congress an arid field of indifference.

Meanwhile, travelers had to be reminded how the railroad time operated and continued to rely on explanations in pocket diaries. The first Baedeker guide to the United States, issued in 1893, devoted to the time zones a paragraph that ended on a querulous note: "in some cases . . . the results are confusing." They were for William Cooper of Elmira, New York, who recalled at ninety-seven his first trip by train, to Chicago, to attend the Columbian Exposition:

"I was early to bed with eagerness. Sleepily in the green curtained booth I got to thinking (11 years old) that the geography showed an hour's change. I kept waking and peeking to see what the country west of Buffalo looked like and when a big old open faced silver watch came to 6, I dressed fast and expected to see Chicago any minute. It was bright dawn before I discovered that we were in the new time zone and that my arithmetic was reversed and when I got up and dressed at my old 6, it was not 7 but 5 o'clock!"

Even more confusing for unwary travelers were the occasional changes in time-zone boundaries. In 1908, after the Eastern zone was extended westward, very close to Detroit, the voters of that city were given a chance to decide on the "kind of time they prefer." A vociferous element argued for rejection of both Eastern and Central standards and a return to local sun time. These zealots insisted that any of their neighbors who were, as the *Times* put it, "violently opposed to the domination of the sun" might as well move to Pittsburgh.

The Detroit incident was one of the last, for in 1908 Parliament considered a bill advancing all British clocks an hour during the summer months, and although it eventually was defeated, it gave an unexpected new direction to the talk about time. The Briton who first proposed the idea, William Willett, tried to drum up American support by writing to every member of Congress, few of whom were much interested. But broad press coverage stimulated general debate on the pros and cons of Willett's summer time, which was quickly dubbed daylight saving.

President Taft, an early convert, publicly urged communities to adopt daylight saving by ordinance, and his hometown of Cincinnati promptly did so. Strong opposition developed elsewhere, however, notable on the editorial pages of *The New York Times,* where it was ridiculed week after week as "an act of madness." We "will have to hear a lot of better arguments than have yet been advanced," an editorial asserted, "before we join enthusiastically in the naive game of playing that 7 o'clock is 8 or 9."

The debate, which continued for almost a decade, was given fresh impetus by America's entry into the European war in 1917. Germany and Great Britain had adopted summertime daylight saving in 1916 as a means of conserving fuel, and this wartime purpose converted even *The New York Times.* The editor warned, however, that it would be effective only if the entire nation was required to advance its clocks uniformly. "and unanimous consent is hard to get, out of the Senate as well as in it."

The warning was justified; short of congressional flat, there could be no hope of nationwide compliance. On Nantucket Island a town meeting voted down a daylight-saving ordinance, and Harvard College students rejected the idea by a vote of 689 to 393. But with the strong endorsement of President Wilson, Congress passed a Daylight Saving Act in 1918 and Wilson affixed his signature on March 20—less than two weeks before clocks were to be advanced. Opponents of daylight saving, and rural diehards who cling to "God's Time," had lost their fight against "Wilson's Time."

In New York City people thronged Madison Square, while at the nearby Aldine Club, Marcus M. Marks, Manhattan's borough president an the nations most energetic campaigner for daylight saving, watched the show outside. At 2:00 A.M. on Sunday, March 31, Marks pushed a button, and the hour hand on the Metropolitan Tower clock moved ahead.

The daylight saving thus welcomed was annulled the very next year, when, with the war ended, conserving fuel no longer seemed essential; nearly half a century would pass before its permanent national adoption in 1966. but the 1918 act contained a clause that at last made standard time official. The members of Congress, in their deliberations, had realized that if all the nation's clocks were to be advanced for part of the year, the base for the advance had to be uniform, and that called for compliance with standard time, compulsory nationwide.

Even today, sixty-five years after Congress finally imposed standard time on the entire nation, not everybody is altogether happy about daylight saving or about the time-zone boundaries. But everyone can appreciate the irony of standard time becoming official only by riding in tardily on the coattails of daylight savings.

The Birth of Jim Crow

C. Vann Woodward

In the spring of 1885, Charles Dudley Warner, Mark Twain's friend, neighbor, and onetime collaborator from Hartford, Connecticut, visited the International Exposition at New Orleans. He was astonished to find that "white and colored people mingled freely, talking and looking at what was of common interest," that Negroes "tooker their full share of the parade and the honors," and that the two races associated "in unconscious equality of privileges." During his visit he saw "a colored clergyman in his surplice seated in the chancel of the most important white Episcopal church in New Orleans, assisting in the service."

It was a common occurrence in the 1800's for foreign travellers and northern visitors to comment, sometimes with distaste and always with surprise, on the freedom of association between white and colored people in the South. Yankees in particular were unprepared for what they found and sometimes estimated that conditions below the Potomac were better than those above. There was discrimination to be sure, and Negroes were often excluded from first-class public accommodations—as they were in the North. But that was done on the responsibility of private owners or managers and not by requirement of law. According to the Supreme Court's decision in the Civil Rights Cases of 1883 the federal law gave no protection from such private acts.

Where discrimination existed it was often erratic and inconsistent. On trains the usual practice was to exclude Negroes from first-class or "ladies' " cars but to permit them to mix with whites in second-class or "smoking" cars. In the old seaboard states of the South, however, Negroes were as free to ride first class as whites. In no state was segregation on trains complete, and in none was it enforced by law. The age of Jim Crow was still to come.

The first genuine Jim Crow law requiring railroads to carry Negroes in separate cars or behind partitions was adopted by Florida in 1887. Mississippi followed this example in 1888; Texas in 1889; Louisiana in 1890; Alabama, Arkansas, Georgia, and Tennessee in 1891; and Kentucky in 1892. The Carolinas and Virginia did not fall into line until the last three years of the century.

Negroes watched with despair while the legal foundations for the Jim Crow system were laid and the walls of segregation mounted around them. Their disenchantment with the hopes based on the Civil War amendments and the Reconstruction laws was nearly complete by 1890. The American commitment to equality, solemnly attested by three amendments to the Constitution and by elaborate civil rights acts, was virtually repudiated. The "compromise of 1877" between the Hayes Republicans and the southern conservatives had resulted in the withdrawal of federal troops from the South and the formal end of Reconstruction. What had started then as a retreat had within a decade turned into a rout. Northern radicals and liberals had abandoned the cause; the courts had rendered the Constitution helpless; the Republican party had forsaken the cause it had sponsored. A tide of racism was mounting in the country unopposed.

The colored community of New Orleans, with its strong infusion of French and other nationalities, was in a strategic position to furnish leadership for the resistance against segregation. Many of these people had culture, education, and some wealth, as well as a heritage of several generations of freedom. Unlike the great majority of Negroes, they were city people with an established professional class and a high degree of literacy. By ancestry as well as by residence they were associated with Latin cultures at variance with Anglo-American ideas of race relations. Their forebears had lived under the Code Noir decreed for Louisiana by Louis XIV, and their city faced out upon Latin America.

When the Jim Crow car bill was introduced in the Louisiana legislature, New Orleans Negroes organized to fight it. Negroes were still voting in large numbers, and there were sixteen colored senators and representatives in the Louisiana General Assembly. On May 24, 1890, that body received "A Protest of the American Citizens' Equal Rights Association of Louisiana Against Class Legislation." An organization of colored people, the association protested that the pending bill was "unconstitutional, unamerican, unjust, dangerous and against sound public policy." It would, declared the protest, "be a free license to the evilly-disposed that they might with impunity insult, humiliate, and otherwise maltreat inoffensive persons, and especially women and children who should happen to have a dark skin."

On July 10, 1890, the Assembly passed the bill, the governor signed it, and it became law. Entitled "An Act to promote the comfort of passengers," the new law required railroads "to provide equal but separate accommodations for the white and colored races." Two members of the Equal Rights Association, L. A. Martinet, editor of the New Orleans *Crusader,* and R. L. Desdunes, placed heavy blame on the sixteen colored members of the Assembly for the passage of the bill. According to Martinet, "they were completely the masters of the situation." They had but to withhold their support for a bill desired by the powerful Louisiana Lottery Company until the Jim Crow bill was killed. "But in an evil moment," he added, "our Representatives turned their ears to listen to the golden siren," and "did so for a 'consideration.' "

Putting aside recriminations, the *Crusader* declared: "The Bill is now a law. The next thing is what we are going to do?" The editor spoke testily of boycotting the railroads, but concluded that "the next thing is . . . to begin to gather funds to test the constitutionality of this law. We'll make a case, a test case, and bring it before the Federal Courts." On September 1, 1891, a group of eighteen men of color formed a "Citizens' Committee to Test the Constitutionality of the Separate Car Law."

Money came in slowly at first, but by October 11, Martinet could write that the committee had already collected $1,500 and that more could be expected "after we have the case well started." Even before the money was collected, Martinet had opened a correspondence about the case with Albion Winegar Tourgée of Mayville, New York, and on October to the Citizens' Committee formally elected Tourgée "leading counsel in the case, from beginning to end, with power to choose associates."

This action called back into the stream of history a name prominent in the annals of Reconstruction. Albion Tourgée was in 1890 probably the most famous surviving carpetbagger. His fame was due not so much to his achievements as a carpetbagger in North Carolina, significant though they were, as to the six novels about his Reconstruction experiences that he had published since 1879. Born in Ohio, of French Huguenot descent, he had served as an officer in the Union Army, and moved to Greensboro, North Carolina, in 1865 to practice law. He soon became a leader of the Radical Republican party, took a prominent part in writing the Radical Constitution of North Carolina, and served as a judge of the superior court for six years with considerable distinction. He brought to the fight against segregation in Louisiana a combination of zeal and ability that the Citizens' Committee of New Orleans would have found it hard to duplicate. They had reason to write him, "we know we have a friend in you & we know your ability is beyond question." He was informed that the committee's decision was made "spontaneously, warmly, & gratefully."

Tourgée's first suggestion was that the person chosen for defendant in the test case be "nearly white," but that proposal raised some doubts. "It would be quite difficult," explained Martinet, "to have a lady *too* nearly white refused admission to a 'white' car." He pointed out that "people of tolerably fair complexion, even if unmistakably colored, enjoy here a large degree of immunity from the accursed prejudice. . . . To make this case would require some tact." He would volunteer himself, "but I am one of those whom a fair complexion favors. I go everywhere, in all public places, though well-known all over the city, & never is anything said to me. On the cars it would be the same thing. In fact, color prejudice, in this respect does not affect me. But, as I have said, we can try it with another."

Railroad officials proved surprisingly co-operative. The first one approached, however, confessed that his road "did not enforce the law." It provided the Jim Crow car and posted the required sign, but told its conductors to molest no one who ignored instruc-

57

tions. Officers of two other roads "said the law was a bad and mean one; they would like to get rid of it," and asked for time to consult counsel. "They want to help us," said Martinet, "but dread public opinion." The extra expense of separate cars was one reason for railroad opposition to the Jim Crow law.

It was finally agreed that a white passenger should object to the presence of a Negro in a "white" coach, that the conductor should direct the colored passenger to go to the Jim Crow car, and that he should refuse to go. "The conductor will be instructed not to use force or molest," reported Martinet, "& *our* white passenger will swear out the affidavit. This will give us our *habeas corpus* case, I hope." On the appointed day, February 24, 1892, Daniel F. Desdunes, a young colored man, bought a ticket for Mobile, boarded the Louisville & Nashville Railroad, and took a seat in the white coach.

All went according to plan. Desdunes was committed for trial to the Criminal District Court in New Orleans and released on bail. On March 21, James C. Walker, a local attorney associated with Tourgée in the case, filed a plea protesting that his client was not guilty and attacking the constitutionality of the Jim Crow law. He wrote Tourgée that he intended to go to trial as early as he could.

Between the lawyers there was not entire agreement on procedure. Walker favored the plea that the law was void because it attempted to regulate interstate commerce, over which the Supreme Court held that Congress had exclusive jurisdiction. Tourgée was doubtful. "What we want," he wrote Walker, "is not a verdict of not guilty, nor a defect in this law but a decision whether such a law can be legally enacted and enforced in any state and we should get everything off the track and out of the way for such a decision." Walker confessed that "it's hard for me to give up my pet hobby that the law is void as a regulation of interstate commerce," and Tourgée admitted that he "may have spoken too lightly of the interstate commerce matter."

The discussion was ended abruptly and the whole approach altered before Desdunes' case came to trial by a decision of the Louisiana Supreme Court handed down on May 25. In this case, which was of entirely independent origin, the court reversed the ruling of a lower court and upheld the Pullman Company's plea that the Jim Crow law was unconstitutional in so far as it applied to interstate passengers.

Desdunes was an interstate passenger holding a ticket to Alabama, but the decision was a rather empty victory. The law still applied to intrastate passengers, and since all states adjacent to Louisiana had by this time adopted similar or identical Jim Crow laws, the exemption of interstate passengers was of no great importance to the Negroes of Louisiana, and it left the principle against which they contended unchallenged. On June 1, Martinet wired Tourgée on behalf of the committee, saying that "Walker wants new case wholly within state limits," and asking Tourgée's opinion. Tourgée wired his agreement.

One week later, on June 7, Homer Adolph Plessy bought a ticket in New Orleans, boarded the East Louisiana Railroad bound for Covington, a destination "wholly within the state limits," and took a seat in the white coach. Since Plessy later described himself as "seven-eights Caucasian and one-eighth African blood," and swore that "the admixture of colored blood is not discernible," it may be assumed that the railroad had been told of the plan and had agreed to co-operate. When Plessy refused to comply with the conductor's request that he move to the Jim Crow car, he was arrested by Detective Christopher C. Cain "and quietly accompanied the officer." The New Orleans *Times-Democrat* remarked that "It is generally believed that Plessy intends testing the law before the courts."

In due course Homer Plessy's case became *Plessy v. Ferguson.* The latter name belonged to John H. Ferguson, Judge of Section A of the Criminal District Court for the Parish of New Orleans, who overruled the plea of Tourgée and Walker, the defendant's counsel, that the Jim Crow law was null and void because it was in conflict with the Constitution of the United States. Plessy then applied to the State Supreme Court for a writ of prohibition and certiorari and was given a hearing in November, 1892. The court recognized that neither the interstate commerce clause nor the question of equality of accommodations was involved and held that "the sole question" was whether a law requiring "separate but equal accommodations" violated the Fourteenth Amendment. Citing numerous decisions of lower federal courts to the effect that accommodations did not have to be identical to be equal, the court as expected upheld the law.

"We have been at pains to expound this statute," added the court, "because the dissatisfaction felt with it by a portion of the people seems to us so unreasonable that we can account for it only on the ground of some misconception."

Chief Justice Francis Redding Tillou Nicholls, heading the court that handed down this decision in 1892, had signed the Jim Crow act as governor when it was passed in 1890. Previously he had served as the "Redeemer" governor who took over Louisiana from the carpetbaggers in 1877 and inaugurated a brief regime of conservative paternalism. In those days Nicholls had denounced race bigotry, appointed Negroes to office, and attracted many of them to his party.

L. A. Martinet wrote Tourgée that Nicholls in those years had been "fair & just to colored men" and had, in fact, "secured a degree of protection to the colored people not enjoyed under Republican Governors." But in November, 1892, the wave of Populist rebellion among the white farmers was reaching its crest in the South, and Judge Nicholls' change of course typified the concessions to racism that conservatives of his class made in their efforts to forestall or divert the rebellion. Nonetheless, at a further hearing Nicholls granted Plessy's petition for a writ of error that permitted him to seek redress before the Supreme Court of the United States.

The brief that Albion Tourgée submitted to the Supreme Court in behalf of Plessy breathed a spirit of equalitarianism that was more in tune with his carpetbagger days than with the prevailing spirit of the mid-nineties.

At the very outset, he advanced an argument in behalf of his client that unconsciously illustrated the paradox that had from the start haunted the American attempt to reconcile strong color prejudice with deep equalitarian commitments.

Plessy, he contended, had been deprived of property without due process of law. The "property" in question was the "reputation of being white." It was "the most valuable sort of property, being the master-key that unlocks the golden door of opportunity." Intense race prejudice excluded any man suspected of having Negro blood "from the friendship and companionship of the white man," and therefore from the avenues to wealth, prestige, and opportunity. "Probably most white persons if given the choice," he held, "would prefer death to life in the United States as *colored persons.*"

Since Tourgée had proposed that a person who was "nearly white" be selected for the test case, it may be presumed that he did so with this argument in mind. But this was not a defense of the colored man against discrimination by whites, but a defense of the "nearly" white man against the penalties of color. The argument, whatever its merits, apparently did not impress the Court.

Tourgée went on to develop more relevant points. He emphasized especially the incompatibility of the segregation law with the spirit and intent of the Thirteenth and particularly the Fourteenth amendments. Segregation perpetuated distinctions "of a servile character, coincident with the institution of slavery." He held that "slavery was a caste, a legal condition of subjection to the dominant class, a bondage quite separable from the incident of ownership." He scorned the pretense of impartiality and equal protection advanced in the defense of the "separate but equal" doctrine.

"The object of such a law," he declared, "is simply to debase and distinguish against the inferior race. Its purpose has been properly interpreted by the general designation of 'Jim Crow Car' law. Its object is to separate the Negroes from the whites in public conveyances for the gratification and recognition of the sentiment of white superiority and white supremacy of right and power." He asked the members of the Court to imagine the tables turned and themselves ordered into a Jim Crow car. "What humiliation, what rage would then fill the judicial mind!" he exclaimed.

The clue to the true intent of the Louisiana statute was that it did not apply "to nurses attending the children of the other race." On this clause Tourgée shrewdly observed:

> The exemption of nurses shows that the real evil lies not in the color of the skin but in the relation the colored person sustains to the white. if he is a dependent it may be endured: if he is not, his presence is insufferable. Instead of being intended to promote the *general* comfort and moral well-being, this act is plainly and evidently intended to promote the happiness of one class by asserting its supremacy and the inferiority of another class. Justice is pictured blind and her daughter, the Law, ought as least to be color-blind.

Tourgée then asked the Court to look to the future. Should the separate-car law by upheld, he inquired, "what is to prevent the application of the same principle to other relations?" Was there any limit to such laws? "Why not require all colored people to walk on one side of the street and whites on the other? . . . One side of the street may be just as good as the other. . . . The question is not as to the *equality* of the privileges enjoyed, but *the right of the State to label one citizen as white and another as colored* in the common enjoyment of a public highway."

The Supreme Court did not get around to handing down a decision on *Plessy v. Ferguson* until 1896. In the years that intervened between the passage of the Louisiana segregation law in July, 1890, and the time of the eventual decision on its constitutionality in 1896, the retreat from the commitment to equality had quickened its pace in the South and met with additional acquiescence, encouragement, and approval in the North. Two states had already disfranchised the Negro, and several others, including Louisiana, were planning to take the same course. In 1892 Congress defeated the Lodge Bill, designed to extend federal protection to elections, and in 1894 it wiped from the federal statute books a mass of Reconstruction laws for the protection of equal rights. And then, on September 18, 1895, Booker T. Washington delivered a famous speech embodying the so-called "Atlanta Compromise," which was widely interpreted as an acceptance of subordinate status for the Negro by the foremost leader of the race.

On May 18, 1896, Justice Henry Billings Brown, a resident of Michigan but a native of Massachusetts, delivered the opinion of the Court in the case of *Plessy v. Ferguson.* His views upholding the defendant's case—that the "separate but equal" doctrine was constitutional—were in accord with those of all his brothers, with the possible exception of Justice David Josiah Brewer, who did not participate, and the certain exception of Justice John Marshall Harlan, who vigorously dissented in phrases that often echoed Tourgée's arguments. In approving, to all intents and purposes, the principle of segregation, Justice Brown followed not only the trend of the times, but a host of state judicial precedents, which he cited at length. That there were no federal judicial precedents to the contrary only added to the technical strength of his position. Just as telling, perhaps, was Brown's mention of the action of Congress in establishing segregated schools for the District of Columbia, an action endorsed by Radical Republicans who had supported the Fourteenth Amendment, and sustained in regular congressional appropriations ever since.

Similar laws, wrote Brown, were adopted by "the legislatures of many states, and have been generally, if not uniformly, sustained by the courts." The validity of such segregation laws, he maintained, depended on their "reasonableness." And in determining reasonableness, the legislature "is at liberty to act with reference to the established usages, customs, and traditions of the people, and with a view to the promotion of their comfort, and the preservation of the public peace and good order."

In addition to judicial precedent and accepted practice, Justice Brown ventured into the more uncertain fields of sociology and psychology for support of his opinion. He wrote:

> We consider the underlying fallacy of the plaintiff's argument to consist in the assumption that the enforced separation of the two races stamps the colored race with a badge of inferiority. If this be so, it is not by reason of anything found in the act, but solely because the colored race chooses to put that construction upon it. . . . The argument also assumes that social prejudices may be overcome by legislation, and that equal rights cannot be secured by the negro except by an enforced commingling of the two races. We cannot accept this proposition. . . . Legislation is powerless to eradicate racial instincts, or to abolish distinctions based upon physical differences, and the attempt to do so can only result in accentuating the difficulties of the present situation. If the civil and

political rights of both races be equal, one cannot be inferior to the other civilly or politically. If one race be inferior to the other socially, the constitution of the United States cannot put them upon the same plane.

One of the most fascinating paradoxes in American jurisprudence is that the opinion of a native son of Massachusetts, Brown, should have bridged the gap between the radical equalitarian commitment of 1868 and the reactionary repudiation of that commitment in 1896; and that Harlan, a southerner, should have bridged the greater gap between the repudiation of 1896 and the radical rededication to the equalitarian idealism of 1868 in 1954. For the dissenting opinion of Justice Harlan, embodying many of the arguments of Plessy's ex-carpetbagger counsel, foreshadowed the Court's eventual repudiation of the *Plessy v. Ferguson* decision and the doctrine of "separate but equal" more than half a century later—a repudiation in which, fittingly enough, Harlan's grandson and namesake on the Warren Court wholly concurred.

The elder John Marshall Harlan is correctly described by Robert Cushman as "a Southern gentleman and a slave-holder, and at heart a conservative." A Kentuckian of the Whig persuasion, Harlan had opposed secession and fought in the Union Army, but at the same time he opposed both the emancipation of the slaves and the passage of civil rights laws to protect the rights of the freedmen. Shocked by Ku Klux excesses, he experienced a sudden conversion, renounced his former views, became a Republican in 1868, and was appointed to the Supreme Court by President Hayes in 1877.

After his conversion Harlan became one of the most outspoken champions of Negro rights of his time, and during this thirty-four years on the bench he lifted his voice repeatedly against denial of those rights by the dominant opinion of the Court. His famous dissent in the Civil Rights Cases of 1883 had denounced the "subtle and ingenious verbal criticism" by which "the substance and spirit of the recent amendments of the Constitution have been sacrificed." And in 1896 he was ready to strike another blow for his adopted cause.

Harlan held the Louisiana segregation law in clear conflict with both the Thirteenth and the Fourteenth amendments. The former "not only struck down the institution of slavery," but also "any burdens or disabilities that constitute badges of slavery or servitude," and segregation was just such a burden or badge. Moreover, the Fourteenth Amendment "added greatly to the dignity and glory of American citizenship, and to the security of personal liberty," and segregation denied to Negroes the equal protection of both dignity and liberty. "The arbitrary separation of citizens, on the basis of race, while they are on a public highway," he said, "is a badge of servitude wholly inconsistent with the civil freedom and the equality before the law established by the constitution. It cannot be justified upon any legal grounds."

Harlan was as scornful as Tourgée had been of the claim that the separate-car law did not discriminate against the Negro. "Every one knows," he declared, that its purpose was "to exclude colored people from coaches occupied by or assigned to white persons." This was simply a poorly disguised means of asserting the supremacy of one class of citizens over another. The Justice continued:

> But in view of the constitution, in the eye of the law, there is in this country no superior, dominant, ruling class of citizens. There is no caste here. Our constitution is color-blind, and neither knows nor tolerates classes among citizens. In respect of civil rights, all citizens are equal before the law. The humblest is the peer of the most powerful. The law regards man as man, and takes no account of his surroundings, or of his color when his civil rights as guarantied by the supreme law of the land are involved. . . . We boast of the freedom enjoyed by our people above all other peoples. But it is difficult to reconcile that boast with a state of law which, practically, puts the brand of servitude and degradation upon a large class of our fellow citizens,—our equals before the law. The thin disguise of "equal" accommodations for passengers in railroad coaches will not mislead any one, nor atone for the wrong this day done.

"The present decision, it may well be apprehended," predicted Harlan, "will not only stimulate aggressions, more or less brutal and irritating, upon the admitted rights of colored citizens, but will encourage the belief that it is possible, by means of state enactments, to defeat the beneficent purpose which the people of the United States had in view when they adopted the recent amendments of the constitution. . . ." For if the state may so regulate the railroads, "why may it not so regulate the use of the streets of its cities and towns as to compel white citizens to keep on one side of a street, and black citizens to keep on the other," or, for that matter, apply the same regulations to streetcars and other vehicles, or to courtroom, the jury box, the legislative hall, or to any other place of public assembly?

"In my opinion," the Kentuckian concluded, "the judgment this day rendered will, in time, prove to be quite as pernicious as the decision made by this tribunal in the Dred Scott Case."

But Harlan was without allies on the Court, and the country as a whole received the news of its momentous decision upholding the "separate but equal" doctrine in relative silence and apparent indifference. Thirteen years earlier the Civil Rights Cases had precipitated pages of news reports, hundreds of editorials, indignant rallies, congressional bills, a Senate report, and much general debate. In striking contrast, the *Plessy* decision was accorded only short, inconspicuous news reports and virtually no editorial comment outside the Negro press. A great change had taken place, and the Court evidently now gave voice to the dominant mood of the country. Justice Harlan had spoken for the forgotten convictions of a bygone era.

The racial aggressions he foresaw came in a flood after the decision of 1896. Even Harlan indicated by his opinion of 1899 in *Cummings v. Board of Education* that he saw nothing unconstitutional in segregated public schools. Virginia was the last state in the South to adopt the separate-car law, and she resisted it only until 1900. Up to that year this was the only law of the type adopted by a majority of the southern states. But on January

12, 1900, the editor of the Richmond *Times* was in full accord with the new spirit when he asserted: "It is necessary that this principle be applied in every relations of Southern life. God Almighty drew the color line and it cannot be obliterated. The negro must stay on his side of the line and the white man must stay on his side, and the sooner both races recognize this fact and accept it, the better it will be for both."

With a thoroughness approaching the incredible, the color line *was* drawn and the Jim Crow principle was applied even in those areas that Tourgée and Harlan had suggested a few years before as absurd extremes. In sustaining all these new laws, courts universally and confidently cited *Plessy v. Ferguson* as their authority. They continued to do so for more than half a century.

On April 4, 1950, Justice Robert H. Jackson wrote old friends in Jamestown, New York, of his surprise in running across the name of Albion W. Tourgée, once a resident of the nearby village of Mayville, in connection with segregation decisions then pending before the Supreme Court. "The *Plessy* case arose in Louisiana," he wrote, "and how Tourgée got into it I have not learned. In any event, I have gone to his old brief, filed here, and there is not argument made today that he would not make to the Court. He says, 'Justice is pictured blind and her daughter, the Law, ought at least to be color-blind.' Whether this was original with him, it has been gotten off a number of times since as original wit. Tourgée's brief was filed April 6, 1896 and now, just fifty-four years after, the question is again being argued whether his position will be adopted and what was a defeat for him in '96 be a postmortem victory."

Plessy v. Ferguson remained the law of the land for fifty-eight years lacking one day, from May 18, 1896, to May 17, 1954, when the Supreme Court as last renounced it in the school segregation cases of *Brown* et al. *v. Board of Education of Topeka,* et al. In that decision could indeed be found, at long last, a vindication, "a post-mortem victory"—not only for the excarpetbagger Tourgée, but for the ex-slaveholder Harlan as well.

Yanks in Siberia

Richard O'Connor

During mid-August, 1918, American forces began landing at Vladivostok, the capital of the Soviet Maritime Territory, in one of the more curious side shows of the First World War. From Moscow it appeared that the United States had joined other western nations and Japan in supporting the White counterrevolution, which just then was making dangerous headway against the Red armies, and on August 30, in a speech before a throng of factory workers, Lenin denounced the United States as a fake democracy standing for the "enslavement of millions of workers."

From a Washington hazed over with Wilsonian rhetoric, about self-determination the perspective was quite different. President Woodrow Wilson wasn't bent on smashing the revolution but, he said, on aiding a force of over forth thousand Czechoslovak soldiers, formerly a unit of the Russian army and now supposedly heading for Vladivostok along the Trans-Siberian railroad, thence to embark for the western front to renew the fight against Germany.

Early in 1918 it was proposed in the Supreme War Council at Versailles that Britain, France, Italy, Japan, and the United States send forces to Russia to re-establish an eastern front against Germany, the new Soviet government having negotiated a separate peace and opted out of the war. The intervention was to be in two widely separated areas, both theoretically propitious to Allied aims: at Murmansk and Archangel in north Russia and at Vladivostok on the Pacific. The Far Eastern intervention proceeded despite warnings that the project would chiefly benefit Japan in its ambitions to expand on the Asian mainland, that Siberia already was a political and military maelstrom in which the various Bolshevik partisan bands, the Russian counter-revolutionary forces soon to be headed by Admiral Kolchak, Cossack regiments turned to brigandage, and a pan-Mongol movement led by a demented Baltic baron all were trying to fill the vacuum caused by the fall of the Romanoffs and the present weakness of the Soviet central government.

Siberia, as viewed from the War Department in Washington, seemed a good place to avoid as far as United States military involvement was concerned. The general staff believed the country had taxed itself to the utmost in sending an expeditionary force to France and had little moral energy or physical reserves to expend on adventures on the other side of the globe.

Only a vague historical memory now, without any great battles or garlanding of sensational headlines, the American intervention in Russia would loom larger in the ensuing half century. In north Russia it resulted in military action that justified a complaint by Nikita Khrushchev in 1959 that "American soldiers were to out soil . . . to help the White Guard combat the new revolution." [See "Where Ignorant Armies Clashed by Night," AMERICAN HERITAGE, December, 1958.] In Siberia it marked the first serious American interference in an Asian land war and was, as John Paton Davies, Jr., recently wrote, the "precursor of Washington's excursions of 1945–49 into the Chinese civil war and, more recently, the civil wars of Indo-China."

But President Wilson, for a complex of reasons that were not altogether clear, created the Siberian Expeditionary Force (S.E.F.) as an act of Presidential will. In falling in with the Anglo-French proposals for the venture he seemed (particularly to Lenin) to be disregarding his own Fourteen Points and his assurance that Russia would have an "unhampered and unembarrassed opportunity" to develop in any way she chose.

Late in June, 1918, Wilson was moved toward taking the step when news, was received from western Siberia that the Czech legion had been attacked by the Red Guards and would have to fight its way eastward along the Trans-Siberian, That, as British Prime Minister Lloyd George later said, was the "determining factor" in the intervention, but President Wilson had discovered another reason in the stockpile of approximately one billion dollars' worth of supplies that the United States had sent to Vladivostok to be used by the prerevolutionary Russian armies against the Germans. An expeditionary force could supposedly reclaim those huge supply dumps before they were seized by either the Red or White partisans—or by the Japanese.

On July 6, Wilson announced to his cabinet that he intended to send an expeditionary force to Siberia, Tapping out an aide-memoire on his own typewriter of July 17, the President formulated the terms on which such a force would operate. The separated Czech detachments would be assisted in linking up and then "get into successful cooperation with their Slavic kinsmen," by which the President meant the Russians, but which kind of Russians—the Reds, the Whites, the Cossack freebooters who were ravaging Siberia—he didn't specify. He also ordered the dispatch of a Noah's ark of civilian helpers including the Y.M.C.A. and the Red Cross, trade experts, agronomists, and labor advisors to work on reviving the Siberian economy.

Wilson completed his plans on August 2, having concluded an agreement with Japan that each country would send seven thousand troops; he ignored the objection of the army chief of staff, General Peyton C. March, that the expedition was a strategic blunder that would provide Japan with a respectable cover for seizing the Russian Far East. The State Department, however, with its strong anti-Bolshevik bias, came down on the side of intervention even after intelligence reports indicated that the Japanese were sending not seven thousand but seventy-two thousand troops into Siberia.

To lead the Siberian Expeditionary Force in operations none could foresee, under circumstances in which the commander's own judgment would have to be relied upon more than any guidance from Washington, the army wisely chose one of its more intelligent and capable general officers. The Siberian Follies of 1919 could have been disastrous directed by a less cool and calculating man than Major General William Sidney Graves. Scholarly-looking, bespectacled, kindly, and considerate (as his staff described him), anything but a martinet, General Graves had a saving sense of humor and a strong sense of humanity. He was a curiously American military type that in a later war would be represented by Omar Bradley.

His career, which included the best military education this century could supply, had not been spectacular. Born during the last year of the Civil War, in Mount Calm, Texas, he was the son of a Baptist minister who had become a Confederate colonel. He had taught school before obtaining a West Point appointment. In the forgotten battle of Caloocan (December 31, 1900) during the Philippine insurrection he had been cited for gallantry in action. For many years after that he was secretary of the general staff. Recently he had been assigned to the command of the 8th Division at Camp Fremont, California.

On the morning of August 2, 1919, Graves was ordered to "take the first and fastest train out of San Francisco" and meet Secretary of War Newton D. Baker in Kansas City. At ten o'clock that night—the style of the United States military establishment was much less pretentious during those pre-Pentagon days—he and Baker conferred briefly while seated on crates in the Kansas City railroad station.

The Secretary of War handed Graves a sealed envelope containing two sheets of paper headed "Aide-Memoire," saying, "This contains the policy of the United States in Russia which you are to follow. Watch your step; you will be walking on eggs loaded with dynamite," and then hurried to catch a train back to Washington.

About all that Graves could make of the Presidential directive was that he was to go to Siberia and stay out of trouble. The necessity of helping the Czech legion was emphasized, but he wasn't supposed to "add to the present sad confusion in Russia." He was to concern himself with "safeguarding the rear of the Czecho-Slovaks," but they had no "rear" in the military sense and were simply strung out along the Trans-Siberian. He was further bewildered by a State Department dispatch warning that "Japan's policy would be to keep the various Russian forces apart and oppose any strong Russian central authority" but offering no advice on how that was to be prevented.

And the War Department, on its part, rose to new heights of ineptness in assigning the components of his expedition. A patchwork brigade of units that had been chasing Filipino guerrillas through the tropical jungle was organized in the Philippines and sent to shiver through the sub-zero winters on the Siberian tundra. Those unfortunates in tropical-weight khaki included the 27th and 31st infantry regiments, a company of telegraphers from the Signal Corps, an ambulance company, and a field hospital. The Philippine regiments were so undermanned they had to be fleshed out with five thousand men from Graves's division in California.

Graves and his headquarters staff landed and Vladivostok on September 1—"pitchforked," as he put it, "into the melee." It was a formerly prosperous European-style city with Victorian architecture and trolley lines, now swarming with adventurers, spies, ex-czarist government officials in their double-breasted frock coats with brass buttons, and thousands of refugees. The cafès and cabarets were thronged with the "scourings of the Far East," and the only saint on the scene was a prostitute named Dizzy Marie who specialized in getting sailors back on their ships.

On the day of Graves's arrival the eastern and western echelons of the Czech legion linked up at Chita on the Trans-Siberian, and the primary stated objective of the S.E.F. appeared to be obviated. Graves's force could have turned around and sailed back to Manila, but Washington felt that other good works might be undertaken—the railroads kept running and the Siberian economy revived.

Graves quickly realized that he had been pitchforked into a situation completely different from the Washington view of what was happening in Siberia. A complex and confusing struggle for power had developed. The Japanese aimed to keep the various contenders at one another's throats while attaining dominance over as much of north-eastern Asia as possible. The French and British military missions were busily promoting the White counter-revolution. The Czechs were settling down in garrisons along the Trans-Siberian and showing no great disposition to return to Europe. Various Cossack desperadoes, most of them subsidized by the Japanese, were carving out bandit empires and occasionally riding out against the growing number of Bolshevik partisan bands. Further to the west, at Irkutsk, Admiral Kolchak had been installed as titular head of a White regime that claimed the right to administer the Siberian provinces.

The American commander knew there was going to be interallied friction the moment he presented himself to General Otani, who announced that he was not only commanding the Japanese forces but was "commander-in-chief of the Allied armies." Graves politely declined to regard Otani as his superior. He had already decided that the only way to stay out of trouble was to maintain a posture of absolute neutrality-no military adventures such as argued by his allies (not only the Japanese but the French and British), no intrigues to promote one political faction or the other.

During his first few days in Siberia Graves learned that the supposedly helpless Czechs had established a "capital" in Irkutsk and were proposing to govern large sections of Siberia under a self-supplied mandate and with Anglo-French encouragement to engage in a war against the Soviet forces along the Volga far to the west. Intelligence officers informed Graves there were twenty-four separate "governments" claiming sovereignty over siberia, with nothing in common but enmity for the Bolshevik regime in Moscow. Shortly before his arrival a plebiscite had been held in Vladivostok with the majority voting, to the embarrassment of the Allies and the various factions they supported, for the Bolsheviks. That vote apparently was an expression of resentment against the old czarist officials who were, as Graves observed, "reaping their revenge of Russians who had dared to act contrary to their beliefs."

United States headquarters were established in a building formerly occupied by a German trading firm, and Graves made an inspection tour of the eastern end of the Trans-Siberian to determine where American troops would be garrisoned. The luckier doughboys occupied a former czarist barracks in Vladivostok, but most were assigned to guarding bridges and depots along the Trans-Siberian and living in boxcars with the wheels removed. Their privations in the forty-below winter temperatures were merely a footnote to the general Siberian agony.

Back home their plight, and the dangerous exposure of American interests in the Siberian intervention, were attracting little attention except among liberal intellectual fascinated by the possibilities of the Russian revolution. National attention was riveted on the climactic battles in northern France and the ensuing armistice. Walter Lippmann as editor of the *New Republic* did warn the President that he should stick to his original position of "no interference in Russia's internal affairs." *The Nation* and other liberal journals joined in that warning, and Justice Louis D. Brandeis wrote to a friend that Wilson "should be judged by what he was and did prior to August 4th, 1918, the date of the paper justifying the attack of Russia. That was the first of his acts which was unlike him; and I am sure the beginning of the sad end."

Although American and Soviet soldiers were indeed killing one another in north Russia, in Siberia, there was no "attack on Russia." An intervention, yes, but otherwise the Americans there presented themselves as peace-keepers and held aloof from the political struggle. General Graves favored neither the Reds nor the Whites. His troops, he told allied officers who tried to pressure him into joining the campaign against the Bolshevik partisan bands, would venture no farther west than Lake Baikal and take part in no "crusade" against Bolshevism.

Certainly from the American viewpoint the anti-Bolshevik Russians were the best propaganda anyone could have devised for Bolshevism. General Gregori Semenov, the commander of an "independent" force based on Chita and largely operating from armored trains, presented himself at United States headquarters. A former Cossack colonel, Semenov was an Asiatic Russian with broad cheekbones, tigerish yellow eyes, and a carefully combed Napoleonic forelock. Early in 1918 he had captured the Soviet garrison at Manchuli and sent its members, beaten half to death, to the nearest Red headquarters; since then his methods had been less forbearing. "A murderer, robber and a most dissolute scoundrel" was Graves's opinion.

With his subsidy of a hundred thousand dollars from the Japanese, Semenov ranged the Trans-Siberian in armored train called *The Destroyer,* His private car was fitted out with Oriental rugs, silk bed sheets, and several mistresses. With members of his Savage Division, Semenov would steam into a settlement and order his Mongol cavalrymen to round up all the inhabitants. The male villagers were mowed down with machine guns and most of the nubile women raped. Then the train would roll on to another helpless village. His brain fevered with vodka and cocaine and flashing with apocalyptic visions, Semenov aimed to establish a new Mongol empire, carved out of Manchuria, Mongolia, and eastern Siberia. Meanwhile he presented himself as an American ally, one, as it turned out, whom the Americans would be eager to disavow when he executed sixteen hundred persons in Adrianoka one day and late in 1918 killed a Swedish physician attached to the International Red Cross.

Semenov, however, was a proper gentleman, compared to two of his collaborators who had served in Semenov's regiment on the Caucasian front against the Germans and Turks. Ivan Kalmikov, ataman of the Ussuri Cossacks, had established himself as "dictator" or Khabarovsk, which was an American garrison town. Soon after the Americans arrived, Kalmikov, who was also on the Japanese payroll, captured a United States patrol and held them on charges of not having Russian passports. They were rescued by another American detachment but not before the prisoners had been severely beaten with Cossack knouts. "The worst scoundrel I ever saw or heard of" was General Graves's verdict. "Kalmikov murdered with his own hands, where Semenov ordered others to kill, and therein lies the difference between Kalmikov and Semenov."

The other Semenov collaborator was a psychopathic sprig of the Baltic nobility named Alexander von Ungern-Sternberg, whom the czar had promoted to major general for his service on the Galician front. Since then the baron had declared himself the reincarnation of Genghis Khan, gathered a following of Mongol horsemen, Cossack adventurers, and Chinese deserters, and seized the Dauria province of Manchuria. A convert to Buddhism, he misconstrued his new religion an sincerely believed that when he killed all Jews he could lay hands on and all people suffering from disease or who were disabled or elderly, he was doing them a favor.

General Graves was so outraged at being forced to witness the depredations of Semenov, Kalmikov, and Ungern-Sternberg that he could only angrily disavow them as collaborators or comrades in arms. The world, he wrote, believed the Siberian Massacres were conducted by Bolshevik partisans, but "the anti-bolsheviks killed one hundred people in eastern Siberia to every one killed by the Bolsheviks."

It was all the more galling that an anti-Bolshevik campaign was being mounted in the United States, and many of his countrymen were urging that he joint the White partisans. Wilson's Attorney General, A. Mitchell Palmer, was imprisoning or deporting thousands suspected of carrying the Communist virus, and many American newspapers, besides supporting those measures, reprinted the statement of Kolchak's liaison officer in Vladivostok that "the United States soldiers are infected with Bolshevism . . . most of them are Jews from the East Side of New York City. . . ." This was, to say the least, a gross exaggeration.

Graves, far from being influenced by the journalistic tom-toms, protested against two incidents that seemed to epitomize the unselective attitude of his government. A representative of the newly organized Siberian cooperatives, which were non-political attempts to revive the Siberian was refused entry by United States immigration authorities, who labelled him a Bolshevik. A few weeks later one of Semenov's lieutenants made the same journey, without Graves's blessing, and was warmly received in Washington. "... One can only assume," Graves wrote, "that character was ignored and political classification alone considered, in determining whether a Russian should be permitted to enter the United States."

As early as November, 1918, the War Department was urging withdrawal of the S.E.F., but President Wilson was preoccupied by the coming peach conference and felt he could not take unilateral action without endangering his plans for the League of Nations; meanwhile dominant elements in the State Department were urging that the S.E.F. support Admiral Kolchak in his expected march on Moscow.

Graves and his troops were increasingly revolted by the activities of Kolchak's forces and their Cossack-Mongol allies; even the hardened veterans of Philippine razzias, in which villages were razed and Moro tribes decimated, found the excesses of Semenov and Kalmikov hard to bear. The populace in and around Khabarovsk repeatedly complained to the American garrison that Kalmikov was kidnapping and murdering everyone he suspected of sympathizing with the Bolsheviks. Just one case in which graves ordered an investigation involved two miners arrested by the ataman. Graves demanded their release, but Kalmikov's Japanese "military adviser" replied that they had escaped. Actually Kalmikov had tied stones around the prisoners' necks and thrown them into a lake. They were among an estimated three hundred persons killed during one of Kalmikov's experiments in terror.

The ataman flogged his own Cossacks in wholesale lots when they rebelled at his liquidation program. Early in 1919 seven hundred of his troopers deserted en masse, about three hundred fleeing into the countryside and three hundred and ninety-eight of them marching in a body to the headquarters of the 27th Infantry in Khabarvsk, where they begged for sanctuary, which was given to them. The Japanese demanded that the deserters be returned to "little father Kalmikov" for paternal correction, but Graves refused and several weeks later released them to go where they pleased.

Aside from demoralization and the threat of political infection of one kind or another, the Americans in Siberia were prey to epidemics ranging in a land where the drinking water came from surface wells. The S.E.F.'S chief surgeon reported to Washington that hundreds had been stricken by "plague, typhus, relapsing fever, typhoid fever, scarlet fever and malignant sore throat."

With each passing month General Graves became more acquainted with the truth of Oscar Wilde's epigram about the pleasures of feasting with panthers: "the danger was half the excitement." The anti-Bolshevik front, he was convinced, was terrorizing the Siberian peasantry in hopes of provoking resistance and thereby "justify calling for more Allied troops to put down the Bolcheviks." The appointment of the old czarist General Ivanoff-Rinoff to organize White forces in the eastern provinces of Amur, Primorskaya, Sakhalin, and Kamchatka seemed an attempt to reimpose czarism without the czar, thereby "delaying the settlement of the Russian question by the Russian people," as Graves put it.

General Ivanoff-Rinoff's brutal procedures convinced him that Semenov and Kalmikov were not atypical representatives of the White cause. in March 1919, American intelligence learned that Ivanoff-Rinoff's troops had dispatched a press gang to the village of Gordyekva. The younger men of the village fled into the forest rather than be forcibly recruited, and ten of the elders were tortured and killed in reprisal. Graves sent one of his staff to investigate. The officer found that the survivors in Gordyekva had armed themselves with old hunting rifles and were prepared to fight to the end if the Ivanoff-Rinoff troops ever reappeared. "General," the officer told Graves on his return to headquarters, "never send me on another expedition like this. I came within an ace of pulling off my uniform, joining those poor people, and helping them as best I could."

Such atrocities the Americans attributed not only to the predictable savagery of a civil war but to the encouragement of the Japanese paymasters. The more trouble the Japanese could foment through their hirelings and the longer the outcome of the Red-White struggle could be delayed, the easier it would be for Imperial Japan to move into the Russian coastal provinces and northern Manchuria. Bolshevik partisans evidently came to the same conclusion as United States intelligence and began ambushing Japanese patrols around Khabarovsk. In February, 1919, two Japanese infantry companies and a battery of field artillery—about four hundred men in all—were attacked by the Bolshevik guerrillas. Only three escaped with their lives. The Japanese liaison officer begged Graves to send a company of United States infantry, but the latter refused with the statement that he would need proof the Japanese had been attacked by partisans rather than Siberian peasants fighting in self-defence. The more violent anti-Communist newspapers in the United States reprinted charges in the Japanese press that Graves had acquiesced in the slaughter of his ally's troops. "Why," Graves effectively replied, "didn't the Japanese send their own troops to the assistance of their men? They had an entire division in Khabarovsk and vicinity, while the Americans had but two battalions."

Graves's resistance to the idea of committing American troops to a shooting war with the Bolsheviks was causing concern among some elements in the State Department and like-minded foreign ministries, but his superior, General March, cabled from Washington, "I am going to stand by you until hell freezes over." The army stood firm against involvement even as the State Department was sending its ambassador to Tokyo, Roland S. Morris, over to Vladivostok to investigate the possibility of American participation in driving the REds back over the Urals.

Despite all the contrary advice from S.E.F. headquarters the United States in mid-1919 decided to support the Kolchak regime in Irkutsk logistically if not, immediately, with military action. A shipment of arms and ammunition was ordered sent from Vladivostok to rearm Kolchak's forces, and a Kolchak emissary appeared at Graves's headquarters with a million dollars in gold to pay for the supplies. The American commander feared, however, that most of the shipment would fall into the hands of Semenov, Kalmikov, and other Japanese-subsidized freebooters and allow them to increase their operations against his scattered garrisons. He halted the transaction on his own initiative, explaining in a cable to Washington, "The Cossacks, under the leadership of Kalmikov, are threatening to commence action against Americans. This action against Americans. This action is supported by Semenov and I believe instigated by Japan. These Cossacks have armored cars which our present arms will not pierce.'' He then requested ''one battalion three-inch or mountain artillery be sent to report to me.''

Thus he was able temporarily to prevent the flooding of Siberia with American arms. His argument that the security of his own forces was paramount to any other considerations could not be debated; his seven-thousand-man force was broken up into many small detachments guarding bridges and other points along a two-thousand-mile section of the Trans-Siberian. If they came under a general attack, the results would be disastrous. A number of incidents indicated the likelihood of such an eventuality. One involved an American soldier waiting in the Vladivostok station for a train to take him back to his unit. An officer in Kolchak's army called him a ''a _____ Bolshevik.'' The American started to swing but was cut down by the Russian's pistol shot. A group of Japanese officers standing nearby went over to congratulate the murderer, who was arrested, tried, acquitted, and released within an hour.

General Graves persisted in his scrupulous neutrality despite attacks from all sides on the Siberian scene and back in the States. The Soviet government failed to appreciate his evenhandedness and rather stupidly charged—and would continue to charge through succeeding decades—that the S.E.F. participated in the plot to restore the Whites to power. Yet only one instance in S.E.F. records can be found in which the American forces operated against the Red partisans in their zone. Bolshevik sympathizers had banded together in the Suchan coal-mining district after being attacked by Kalmikov's irregulars. The Americans had to prevent any large-scale outbreak around the mines because the coal was needed for heating and for keeping the Trans-Siberian operating. They drove the Cossacks out of the district, then engaged in brief skirmishing with bolshevik sympathizers. Otherwise there was no combat between the S.E.F. and regular of irregular forces of the Moscow government.

After stalling as long as he could, General Graves was finally forced to resupply Kolchak, but he agreed to turn over the munitions only in Irkutsk, so that the guns would take longer to filter into the hands of Semenov and his lieutenants. The shipment left Vladivostok in two long trains. One reached Irkutsk without incident. The second, however, was stopped at Chita, Semenov's headquarters, on October 24, 1919. Semenov boarded the train and demanded of the guard detachment's officer, lieutenant Ryan, that he hand over fifteen thousand rifles. Ryan refused, though he had only fifty soldiers to back up his defiance. Semenov replied with an ultimatum: hand over the rifles within thirty hours or be massacred. One armored train pulled up to block the munitions train from the west, another from the east. A Cossack battalion completed the encirclement.

Ryan wired Vladivostok for instructions. Don't give up a single rifle, he was ordered, and open fire if attacked. Ryan and his troopers sweated out the deadline, then ten hours more, before Semenov stopped blustering and allowed the train to proceed.

Graves's suspicion that the arms shipment would be villainously employed was confirmed almost immediately. Through a Russian agent he learned that Kolchak turned over four carloads of weapons to the Cossacks. Shortly thereafter the recipients of those weapons conducted a pogrom in the Ekaterinburg district in which a reported three thousand Jews were massacred. The American liaison officer at Kolchak's headquarters, on questioning how the United States arms were used, was told only that ". . . something . . . occurred at Ekaterinburg that would give the Jews something to think about."

Whatever hopes the more fervent anti-Bolshevik officials in the Wilson administration nurtured that the Siberian expedition might be guided from peace-keeping to crusading under the Whites' banners were blown away toward the end of 1919. In north Russia the Allied invasion force had given up and gone home. The facade of the White counterrevolution in Irkutsk had begun crumbling by the time General Graves made an inspection trip along the Trans-Siberian in the fall. The White armies had become what Graves called a "retreating mob," with long trains heading east, their cars crammed with soldiers suffering from wounds or disease. The law of the jungle, Graves reported, now ruled the Siberian tundra. On December 27 he recommended the immediate withdrawal of the S.E.F.

Three weeks passed before the War Department cabled permission to withdraw. Evacuation would be a delicate and dangerous process because of the far-scattered deployment of the American forces. Just how touchy the situation had become, with Semenov, Kalmikov, and company itching to send the S.E.F. on its way with a bloody nose, was indicated by the Posolskaya incident shortly before Washington approved of the withdrawal.

On January 9, 1920, Semenov's chief lieutenant, General Bogomolets, was terrorizing towns along the American sector of the Trans-Siberian. His armored train was *The Destroyer,* Semenov's personal conveyance, and it roared into Verkhne-Udinsk to arrest the stationmaster because he had protested the seizure of American property. A detachment of United States infantry arrived from the nearby post just in time to prevent the stationmaster from being executed.

In a violently anti-American mood General Bogomolets then steamed sixty miles west to the desolate station of Posolskaya, where Lieutenant Paul Kendall and thirty-eight enlisted men stood guard. The American were attacked by cannon and machine-gun fire from the armored train as they slept in a wooden railway car that had been converted into their barracks. Though heavily outnumbered and badly outgunned, Kendall and his troopers tumbled out of their shelter and into the subarctic night to attack the train with rifles and grenades.

A United States sergeant dashed up to the locomotive of *The Destroyer* and dropped a grenade into its boiler before he was fatally wounded. With doughboys swarming all over his armored cars and firing through the slits of his turrets, Bogomolets lost interest in the battle and called for a withdrawal.

His engineer managed to get up just enough steam for *The Destroyer* to crawl away like a gravely wounded snake. Three miles up the line, hotly pursued by enraged Americans, Bogomolets ran up the white flag. A greater humiliation came with the discovery that twelve of his Cossacks and deserted during the battle. Five others had been killed (to two Americans), and seven Cossack officers (including Bolomolets) and sixty-six men surrendered. Then the train and its whole cutthroat crew were taken in two back to Verkhne-Udinsk.

The expeditionary force thus ended its year and a half of largely peaceful occupation of eastern Siberia on a victorious note. Graves and his staff embarked with the final echelon on April 1, 1920, after he and his G-2, colonel Robert Eichelberger, who twenty-odd years later would command an army under MacArthur in the Southwest Pacific, made a final inspection of the outskirts of Vladivostok. Along the slope above the First River they say Japanese troops building fortifications and settling down for a long stay (but not as long as they planned; under Soviet pressure they withdrew from Siberia in October, 1922). As the last American transport sailed out of the Vladivostok harbor the soldiers on deck heard a Japanese band serenading their departure from the docks. The tune was ''Hard Times Come Again No More.''

Graves and his command had performed a difficult, almost impossible, task with great forbearance and honor. It is easy to imagine the consequences if he had been a glory hunter or one who succumbed to political and journalistic pressures. He believed that 90 per cent of the Siberian populace was anti-Kolchak and anti-czarist—though *not* pro-Bolshevik—and that any aggressive action by the American forces would have resulted in a protracted struggle which a disillusioned America would not have borne without violent dissension. his own career continued on an unspectacular trajectory—command of troops in the Philippines and the Panama Canal Zone—until he retired in 1928 to tend his garden in Shrewsbury, New Jersey, and write his memoirs. He died in 1940.

There was a bitter footnote to the Siberian venture and the passions it aroused. On their return to their homeland Graves and his comrades were accused repeatedly of having favored the Bolshevik cause and of having let out allies down by refusing to join in a crusade beside the disintegrating White forces.

Such charges evidently were taken seriously in the upper reaches of the Harding administration. One evening in November, 1921, General Graves, Admiral Austin Knight (commander of the Asiatic Fleet when it was providing naval support for the S.E.F.), and about sixty other Siberian veterans held a reunion banquet at the Commodore Hotel in New York. A stranger who appeared, uninvited, at the banquet table was asked to identify himself. The gate-crasher showed a Department of Justice badge and muttered threats about what would happen if he were asked to leave. General Graves, who had carried out with skill and moral courage one of the most difficult missions ever given a United States general officer, was ''mortified'' that his own government should feel compelled to spy on him. It was, one is tempted to say today, the shape of things to come.

Mr. Coolidge's Jungle War

Richard O'Connor

The United States was first introduced to the vexations of large-scale guerrilla warfare forty years ago in the mountain jungles of Nicaragua. There for the first time Americans were confronted by an elusive partisan leader of a type to become bitterly familiar not only in the Caribbean but in Southeast Asia, a man who pioneered techniques of warfare when Che Guevara and Fidel Castro were in rompers and Mao Tse-tung was an obscure revolutionary. "Mr. Coolidge's War," the affair has been called. More formally, it was the American intervention in Nicaragua of 1927–28—and thought it was not one of the thunderclaps of history, its significance is evident.

For well over a year a particularly agile and mischievous guerrilla chieftain named Sandino—the name became almost a household word in the late twenties—campaigned successfully against the elite battalions of the United States Marine Corps. In giving them so much trouble, he unintentionally made his country a proving ground for U.S. weapons and tactics. In Nicaragua the Marine Corps began to formulate the doctrine that would guide the jungle campaigns against the Japanese in World War II and against the Viet Cong in South Vietnam; it tried out such novelties as dive-bombing, aerial support of ground forces, search-and-destroy missions, and the counterambush. It would not be appropriate to belabor the point, but with a change of dateline many of the dispatches from Vietnamese battlefields read like the afteraction reports of the Marines' provisional brigade in Nicaragua.

Similarly interchangeable would be the protests of liberal and pacifist elements in the United States. President Coolidge had his Senator Fulbright in the liberal Republican William E. Borah of Idaho, who kept demanding to know the true casualty figures of the U.S. force and of those opposed to it. Another senator introduced a resolution that would have forbidden the President to employ military forces when ''Congress has not declared a state of war to exist.'' Hundreds of ordinary citizens picketed the White House with signs reading ''Wall Street and not Sandino is the Real Bandit,'' and Marines bound for Nicaraguan duty received letters urging them to desert when they landed and join Sandino in his ''war for freedom.''

It was not primarily Wall Street's interests, nor any fervor for foreign ventures on the part of the lackadaisical Coolidge, nor even an ironclad interpretation of the Monroe Doctrine that propelled the intervention. For almost a century the United States had considered Nicaragua strategic to the national interest: it offered the best alternative route for a trans-Isthmus canal—a route that is still a matter of consideration in the event that political upheaval, or the need for a larger canal, should make an alternative to the Panama Canal necessary.*

This continuing strategic interest, plus the concessions obtained by American companies for the exploitation of Nicaragua's bananas, mahogany, and gold, made the country almost an American protectorate. Between 1912 and 1925, Marines were landed several times to restore order after political disturbances. The closely drawn struggle between the Liberal and the Conservative parties in Nicaragua, which had been going on since early in the nineteenth century, erupted with even greater violence late in 1926 when a Conservative, Adolfo Diaz, was elected to the presidency by the Nicaraguan congress and recognized by the United States and most of the other great powers. The Liberal leader, Dr. Juan Sacasa, then proclaimed himself president, with the support of revolutionary forces under General Josè Maria Moncada. Mexico recognized Sacasa and sent him four shiploads of arms and supplies. Before long, his forces had occupied large sections of the country.

Once again the U.S. government felt it was necessary to intervene. The 5th Marine Regiment was landed on the Atlantic coast, and a shore party from the cruiser *Galveston* on the Pacific. The State Department gave the Associated Press a story pointing to the ''spectre of a Mexican-fostered Bolshevistic hegemony intervening between the United States and the Panama Canal.'' By March of 1927 the U.S. Navy reported that 5,414 men were on duty in or en route to Nicaragua. However, President Coolidge decided to make a last try at a political solution. He rushed former Secretary of War Henry L. Stimson to the embattled country aboard a cruiser just as General Moncada's revoluntionary forces advanced to within forty miles of Managua, the capital.

Colonel Stimson briskly set about negotiating a truce between the contending factions. He persuaded President Diaz to offer the rebels a general amnesty, the return of confiscated property, and participation in the Diaz cabinet by Liberal leaders. Then Stimson arranged a meeting with General Moncada, which was held on May 4, 1927, under a large blackthorn tree just outside the village of Tipitapa. A week later they met there again. As a

*A survey of the Nicaraguan route, undertaken by a commission set up by the U.S. Congress in 1938, estimated that such a canal would cost almost $1,500,000,000, against the $375,000,000 spent in Panama. Today, of course, it would cost much more.

result, Moncada agreed to allow Diaz to stay in the presidency provided that the United States would supervise the election the following year.

The various rebel commanders, as requested, signed an agreement with General Moncada that they would surrender their arms—all but one, namely Augusto Sandino. The only word from Sandino was a not saying that he was going north to collect arms from his dissident followers and would "remain there awaiting your [Moncada's] orders." No one paid much attention to Sandino's absence as the various revolutionary battalions and the government forces surrendered their arms to officers of the 5th Marine Regiment. The job of policing the country was assumed by the Marines' provisional brigade and the Nicaraguan constabulary, which was to be commanded by Marine officers.

On May 15, Stimson confidently telegraphed the State Department: "The civil war in Nicaragua is now definitely ended. . . . I believe that the way is now open for the development of Nicaragua along the lines of peace, order, and ultimate self government."

The next day two Marines, Captain Richard B. Buchanan and Private Marvin A. Jackson, were killed when a guerrilla band attacked their post guarding the railroad near León.

Sandino had spoken. It was the starting gun of a long and bitter struggle to pacify the country. Stimson later recorded that General Moncada had told him that Sandino, "having promised to join in the settlement, afterward broke his word and with about 150 followers, most of whom he said were Honduran mercenaries, had secretly left his army and started northward toward the Honduras border."

Stimson left Managua that day, May 16, to return to Washington, convinced that Sandino and his band would soon be tracked down and captured. Instead, the marine Corps, along with the Nicaraguan constabulary, found itself plunged into a guerrilla war with few guidelines and even fewer omens of success.

There were, to be sure, certain precedents. The Marines themselves had been engaged in police actions in Haiti. The U.S. Army, confronted on several occasions by guerrillas of various types, had learned and then forgotten the lesson that it takes a vast preponderance of men and materials to hunt down determined bands of partisans operating in rough country, among people friendly to the quarry but hostile to the hunters. During the Civil War the Union Army had been bedevilled by the irregular forces of Mosby, Quantrill, and others. In 1886 the regular Army had turned out 5,000 of its best troops to run down the Apache leader Geronimo and his followers, whose strength was approximately one per cent of their own. In the southern Philippines after the Spanish-American War, it had taken the army fourteen years to pacify the Moro *insurrectos*. An even more frustrating experience was General John J. Pershing's futile expedition into Mexico in 1916, chasing after Pancho Villa with the best of the U.S. Cavalry and coming back with an empty cage.

Sandino, as Marine intelligence officers quickly learned, meant to stir up as much trouble as possible. He had taken his hard-core followers up into the heavily forested mountains of Nueva Segovia and Jinotega provinces near the Honduras border and was recruiting what became a striking force estimated at one thousand men. He had even designed a battle flag of red and black emblazoned with a death's-head. It was also observed that he was adept at rousing the patriotic emotions of the people in the back country by playing on resentment of foreign violations of their native soil, an emotion stronger in the mountains than in the more sophisticated cities to the south.

Augusto Sandino was a mestizo, not much over five feet tall, with a striking look of self-confidence in his intense black eyes. In 1927 he was thirty-four years old. The son of the owner of a small coffee plantation, he was educated at the Eastern Institute in Granada, worked on his father's *finca,* and then left his native Niquinohomo after a violent dispute with a prominent man in the vicinity. For a time he worked in mines and on banana plantations in Nicaragua, and then he went to Mexico and was employed by an American oil company in Tampico. He returned to his father's home in 1926, laden with books on sociology and syndicalism—and, oddly enough, a bulky missionary tract, which he frequently consulted, published by the Seventh-day Adventists.

He loved to coin heroic slogans and hurl them at his followers on all suitable occasions ("Death is but one little moment of discomfort; it is not to be taken too seriously . . . God and our mountains fight for us"). But Sandino also had a sense of humor. Whenever he "requisitioned" supplies for his forces from the merchants, plantations, or mining companies on which he periodically descended, he insisted with sardonic punctilio on leaving nicely printed certificates: "The Honorable Calvin Coolidge, President of the United States of North America, will pay the bearer $_____."

Sandino's objectives were succinctly stated in a message he left at the La Luz mines after levelling the American-owned property there: "The most honorable resolution which your government could adopt in the conflict with Nicaragua is to retire its forces from our territory, thus permitting us, the Nicaraguans, to elect our national government, which is the only means of pacifying the country. With your government rests the conservation of good or bad relations with our government and you, the capitalists, will be appreciated and respected by us according as you treat us as equals and not in the mistaken manner which now obtains, believing yourselves lords and masters of our lives and property."

The mordant edge of Sandino's humor was soon felt by Marine Captain G. D. Hatfield, whose force of thirty-seven Marines and forty Nicaraguan constables occupied Ocotal, the largest town in the province of Nueva Segovia, and formed the spearhead of the forces charged with running down the rebel. Captain Hatfield and Sandino exchanged a number of letter inviting each other to surrender or, failing that, to "come out and fight." Sandino easily outdid the Marine commander in bravura. One of his messages was decorated with a drawing of a guerrilla brandishing a machete over the prostrate form of a Marine; it was signed, "Your obedient servant, who wishes to put you in a handsome tomb with flowers." Meanwhile, Sandino was striking hard at foreign-owned mining properties in the northern mountains. The managers of French and German mines near Ocotal were kidnapped and held for $5,000 ransom. Sandino and his followers also wrecked the gold mine operated by Charles Butters, an American, at San Albino, where Sandino had worked as a clerk just before joining the Liberal revolution.

On July 15, on orders from his superiors, Captain Hatfield sent Sandino an ultimatum demanding that he surrender within twenty-four hours or be wiped out. "I will not surrender," Sandino replied, "and will await you here. I want a free country or death."

Actually he had already decided against "awaiting" the Marines in the mountains above Ocotal and had begun deploying for an attack. One day after receiving the ultimatum, at 1 A.M. on July 16, he launched a furious assault on the garrison at Ocotal with an estimated six hundred followers. Only luck saved Captain Hatfield and his men from destruction. A Marine sentry patrolling one hundred yards from the city hall sighted a shadow moving along a line of bushes. The shadow, startled, fired on him. The Marine raced to the city hall, where Hatfield's headquarters were located, and the town's defenders were alerted just before Sandino struck in force. The Sandinistas had infiltrated the town and were closing in on the main defense positions around the city hall.

Outnumbered by almost ten to one, the Marines and the constables reacted with admirable discipline and poured rifle, grenade, and machine-gun fire on the attackers from the rooftops, courtyards, and windows. One group of Sandino's men charged into the courtyard behind the city hall and killed a Marine, but was forced to withdraw. In the square fronting on Hatfield's command post, the partisans were caught in a crossfire between Marines in the city hall and the Guardia (constabulary) in the nearby church tower. Thomas G. Bruce, a Marine first sergeant commissioned as a lieutenant in the Guardia, lay in the street behind a heavy machine gun and accounted for many of the Sandinistas trying to cross the square.

At dawn, Sandino realized his surprise attack had failed, and he withdrew his followers from the center of town. The garrison, he decided, would have to be starved out. A heavy fire was poured at long range into the two buildings held by Hatfield and his men.

Two Marine reconnaissance planes, part of the nine-plane unit of World War I de Havillands based in a cow pasture outside Managua, happened to fly over Ocotal late that morning on a routine patrol. On glimpsing the battle below they streaked for their base. At three o'clock that afternoon a flight of five planes led by Major Ross E. Rowell swooped out of rainy skies and proceeded to demonstrate what air support could accomplish even in what the Marines called a "bamboo war." Major Rowell and his flight loosed small bombs and strafed Sandino's positions for a half hour before running out of ammunition.

At nightfall, Captain Hatfield was able to report that Ocotal's defenders had given Sandino a sharp setback. His own casualties included one Marine killed and two wounded and four members of the Guardia wounded, against reports from residents of the town that forty of Sandino's followers had been killed and an unknown number wounded.

Sandino, at any rate, was forced to lift the siege and pull back into the mountains to the east when a column of Marine reinforcements arrived. Several days later he issued a proclamation that he had attacked Ocotal to "prove that we prefer death to slavery" and added that "whoever believes we are downcast by the heavy casualties misjudges my army ..." Another column of Marines and Guardia was sent into the mountainous heart of guerrilla country and occupied the village of Jícaro, which Sandino had renamed Sandino City and designated as his "capital."

The guerrillas had scattered in the mountains in what would become known as a classic pattern of dispersal following an engagement. At the time, however, the American authorities simply took the dispersal as a sign that they were giving up the fight. So convinced were the Americans that Sandino was beaten that they ordered a withdrawal of part of the provisional brigade to Guantánamo in Cuba and to other bases. General Logan Feland also left, after handing over command of the Nicaragua field force to Colonel Louis Mason Gulick. Meanwhile an Army general, Frank R. McCoy, arrived with orders from President Coolidge to supervise the coming election.

The countryside was fairly quiet that summer, and by the end of July there were only 1,700 Marines still stationed in Nicaragua. But the lull was deceptive. Actually Sandino was quietly building up his forces for renewed and heavier fighting. A Marine Corps historian wrote later:

> He was a master of propaganda and managed to use the Ocotal affair to his advantage: it served to attract the attention of communistic and other radical elements in Central America, Mexico and even in the United States; and it made Sandino a central figure to rally around. Considerable sums of money were raised, some even in the United States, and turned over to him for the purpose of providing military equipment and maintaining an armed force. Within a few months Sandino had several thousand followers and an actual armed force of almost a thousand. All this went on, however, without the knowledge of any responsible American official.

Harold Denny, the *New York Times's* capable young man on the scene, agreed that Sandino may have become a hero abroad through "extravagantly false" propaganda, but in Denny's view "he did not represent public opinion in Nicaragua." His countrymen sympathized with Sandino but seldom offered their voluntary support. Many foreigners in Nicaragua, not including Americans, also sympathized with him because

> he was an under dog making a terrific fight. I have heard foreigners in fear of an imminent attack on their plantations discuss him with something akin to admiration. But few people in Nicaragua were really interested in throwing the Americans out of the country, even though they might not love them. To the more intelligent persons of both parties, Sandino was a lively danger to Nicaragua's hard won opportunity for a just peace. Toward the last even some of his supporters outside the country urged him to cease fighting because his warfare, instead of driving the marines from the country, was insuring that they would remain.

The only American to wangle a personal interview with Sandino during the year of his most intense activity as a guerrilla chieftain was Carleton Beals, a correspondent for the *Nation,* one of the most eloquent of the defenders of Sandino's right to foment a rebellion against the American presence. Beals made a long and perilous journey through Honduras and across the northern border of Nicaragua, entering Sandino country through the back door. Through his well-advertised sympathies Beals was enabled to "make the proper connections in Mexico and Guatemala" and follow "the thread of Sandino's underground with the outside world," through El Salvador and then Honduras. While traveling that clandestine route, guided by Sandino sympathizers, Beals was shown a photograph of the town of Chinandega after it was bombed by U.S. planes, and in his report there are foreshadowings of Harrison Salisbury's dispatches from Vietnam. "An entire street laid in ruins and sprinkled with mangled bodies," Beals wrote; "the tumbled walls of the hospital, broken bodies of patients flung about. . . . Was it so long ago that we called the Germans Huns for destroying civilian populations without mercy?"

Beals's interview with Sandino demonstrated to Americans that he was no mere adventurer but a man of intensely idealistic convictions. Sandino attacked the Diaz government as an American puppet, blamed American financial interests for all the troubles visited upon his country, inveighed against Nicaragua's sale of its canal rights to the United States, and blamed the country's economic plight on eighteen years of American intervention. Only in relating his military successes, Beals thought, was Sandino "quite too flamboyant and boastful."

One myth exploded by Beals was the much repeated charge that Sandino was being equipped with Russian arms. Beals examined some of the rifles carried by the Sandinistas and found that they did indeed bear Russian markings. Investigation showed, however, that they had been manufactured in the United States for export to the Kerensky regime, which gave way to the Bolsheviks before the weapons could be employed against the Germans; subsequently they were sold as army surplus to mexico, and were among the four boatloads of arms that Mexico sent to the Liberal revolutionaries just before the Nicaraguan revolution broke out. Beals was not impressed with their quality, observing that some of them "exploded in the hands of the users."

It was Marine air reconnaissance that finally tipped off the American authorities that a new Sandino build-up was in progress. The "squadron" in the Managua cow pasture had been reinforced with new Corsair fighter planes, forerunners of the Navy's World War II carrier planes, and they kept a close surveillance over the mountains of Nueva Segovia province where Sandino was presumed to be hiding. In mid-October it finally became apparent to the Marine headquarters in Managua that their field commanders were right: Sandino was about to stir up trouble again.

The Marine aviators flying over the mountains of Nueva Segovia observed much activity on the trails. In October a plane piloted by Lieutenant Earl A. Thomas, with Sergeant Frank E. Dowdell as his observer, crashed near Quilali in the heart of Sandino country. The pilot of another plane in the same flight saw the two men crash-land and escape from the wreckage. A patrol was sent out to rescue them but became engaged in a heavy fire fight with an estimated three hundred guerrillas; the patrol was forced to withdraw after three of its men were killed. Marine intelligence officers later learned that Thomas and Dowdell were killed by Sandinistas after they took refuge in a cave.

About that time the Marines managed, from aerial reconnaissance and other reports, to pinpoint the center of Sandino activity. It was a mile-high, heavily forested mountain named El Chipote—meaning in Spanish slang "back-handed slap"—in southeastern

Nueva Segovia. The mountain was fifteen miles long and shaped like a battleship. On its prow Sandino had established a fortified camp scored with trenches and pitted with foxholes and machine-gun nests. The Coco River flowed down just to the south of the summit of El Chipote, the Jícaro through a valley on its western flank.

Rooting Sandino out of that stronghold became the Marines' immediate objective. On December 21, 1927, two columns set out on converging marches toward the fortified hogback of El Chipote. They were curiously undermanned, considering the fact that Marine intelligence credited Sandino with having close to a thousand men under his command. One column—one hundred fifty Marines, seven members of the Guardia, and a long pack train, commanded by Captain Richard Livingston—marched from Jinotega; another column, commanded by First Lieutenant Merton A. Richal and consisting of sixty Marines and constabulary, set out from Pueblo Nuevo. They were to meet at Quilali on the Jícaro River and join forces for the climb up El Chipote.

By the morning of December 30, both columns were within a few miles of Quilali. Suddenly Sandino's followers, awaiting their foes' slow and ponderous approach, sprang a double ambush. Less than a mile south of Quilali, as it proceeded along a narrow trail clinging to the flank of El Chipote, Captain Livingston's column was attacked by a large force of Sandinistas from concealed positions above the trail. The guerrillas rained down fire from automatic rifles and trench mortars. (The mortars, homemade, had been produced by Sandino's armory at the Butters mine a few miles up the Jícaro. They were fashioned from lengths of iron pipe, and the missiles they fired were rawhide pouches packed with scraps of iron, stones, and glass fragments; the pouches were tamped into the pipes with charges of dynamite.) Before the column could fights its way out of the trap, give Marines were killed and twenty-three others wounded, six of them, including Captain Livingston, seriously. Their pack train was scattered and most of their supplies lost. Livingston's second-in-command, Lieutenant Moses J. Gould, took over the job of leading the detachment to the village of Quilali through snipers' fire on both sides of the trail.

A short time later the other column was similarly surprised a few miles west of Quilali. It took that detachment two days to fight its way out of a succession of ambushes; Lieutenant Richal himself was seriously wounded and three other Marines were also hit before they reached Quilali. Lieutenant Bruce, the machine gunner who had fought so valiantly at Ocotal, now commanded Richal's Guardia detachment; he was killed in one of the running battles.

The remains of the two columns barricade themselves in the score of stone-walled and tile-roofed houses of Quilali; between them they could muster less than two hundred men able to shoulder arms. Against them were an estimated seven hundred guerrillas who had obviously been trained to a pitch far above that of the usual Central American bush army. The village was under constant fire. Its defenders would be starved out unless relief arrived in a hurry.

Once again it was the fledgling Marine air power, represented by the two-seater Corsairs and obsolescent de Havillands under Major Rowell's command at Managua, that was called upon to balance the odds. Planes on constant reconnaissance over rebel territory spotted the fighting at Quilali. Lieutenant Gould, now in command of the combined ground force, strung messages on wires stretched between two poles, which the pilots picked off with grappling hooks. Among other things, Gould asked if his wounded could be evacuated.

A dashing and skillful pilot, Lieutenant Christian F. Schilt, volunteered to fly out from Managua, land at Quilali, and remove the wounded—or at least try to. Meanwhile Gould and his men hacked out a landing strip. The only possible place where Schilt could land his Corsair was on the three-hundred-foot stretch of the road that ran through the village. Houses on both sides of the road were demolished and cleared away. Then, with picks and shovels dropped by other planes, Gould and his men widened the strip to seventy feet. Lieutenant Schilt would have to land on and take off from a rough patch of ground about the size of a football field.

Somehow Schilt managed to pull off the evacuation despite intense harassing fir from Sandino's men in the surrounding hills. Another Marine pilot circled overhead and poured machine-gun fire into Sandino's positions while Schilt made ten nerve-shredding landings in the besieged village, took out ten of the most seriously wounded, and brought in supplies and a relief officer; it was one of the greatest flying feats of all time. Schilt was awarded the Congressional Medal of Honor.

The Marine air unit continued to support the detachment at Quilali by dropping ammunition and supplies, and by strafing the enemy positions. Captain R. W. Peard, the officer flown in by Lieutenant Schilt, took over the command and moved it to the San Albino mine, a more suitable base for operations against Sandino's camp on the mountain towering over them. Two relief columns under Major Archibald Young also arrived, by truck and on foot. On January 14, 1928, Captain Peard led his command up the trails leading to the summit of El Chipote, supported by a flight of dive-bombing planes, and captured one of Sandino's outposts. The guerrillas' camp itself was repeatedly bombed and strafed. On January 26, Major Young's reinforcements joined them and the combined force attacked Sandino's headquarters—and found it empty.

The moment that news of the heavy fighting at the base of El Chipote was received at Washington, orders were given for a heavy reinforcement of the Marine units in Nicaragua. General Feland was restored to command there, and rifle battalions sailed once again from Guantánamo and other bases until there were 5,700 Marines on the scene. The build-up came at an embarrassing time for the United States. It was the eve of the Pan-American Congress at Havana, and many Latin-American nations were restive over the American intervention. The State Department defended the increase of troops in Nicaragua by declaring that Sandino's guerrillas were ''regarded as ordinary bandits, not only by the Government of Nicaragua, but by both political parties in that country,'' and that American forces would stay only long enough to make certain that a free and fair election would be held. At the conference the delegates of Mexico and El Salvador tried to bring the Nicaraguan question to the floor but were outmaneuvered by the U.S. delegate, former Secretary of State Charles Evans Hughes.

Meanwhile, the Marines and their Guardia allies were launching intensive efforts to catch Sandino and stamp out his rebellion. The northern area, comprising Nueva Segovia province and the adjoining territory where Sandino's bands were handed over to Colonel Robert H. Dunlap and his 11th Marine Regiment to be pacified. His patrols moved throughout Sandino country, often supplied from the air by newly arrived Fokker transport planes. On February 27, 1928, a Marine patrol was ambushed in southern Nueva Segovia: five were killed and eight wounded before a relief column rescued them.

Several weeks later it appeared that Sandino was making a push toward Matagalpa and its coffee plantations. At the head of 150 mounted guerrillas, he occupied the large *finca* of Charles Potter, an Englishman, appropriated all the cash and supplies on the premises, enlisted a number of Potter's workers, and then amiably enough departed. Socres of refugees from the district fled to Matagalpa for protection, since it was guarded by a Marine outpost of forty-five men. Undoubtedly Sandino could have taken the two the night after he left Potter's plantation, though a battalion of Marines was being rushed there in commandeered automobiles. Instead, Sandino and his mounted force vanished in the direction of the northern mountains. Evidently he intended to employ hit-and-run tactics, in the style that would become classic when codified by Mao Tse-tung and Che Guevara. Sandino hoped to keep the country in a turmoil and prevent any American-supervised elections.

Gradually, however, the Americans succeeded in bringing most of the countryside under control, particularly in the north, where Sandino had been able to operate almost at will. Vigorous and constant patrol action, along with the systematic destruction of Sandino's supply caches, whittled down the guerrilla leader's freedom of movement. Suddenly, however, there was an outbreak of banditry on the easter coast of Nicaragua, which had been quiet all through Sandino's activity. In April, a bandit gang raided an American-owned mine, took $12,000 in cash, and kidnapped the manager.

To combat this new menace the Coco Patrol was established under Captain Merritt A. "Red Mike" Edson, who became renowned as a tactician in the jungle campaigns against the Japanese fifteen years later. The patrol, on foot and in boats, moved up and down the Coco River from the eastern lowlands to the uplands of the northwest, where it linked up with patrols from Colonel Dunlap's 11th Regiment. On several occasions Captain Edson's special force outwitted and outfought the bandits who tried to ambush it along the jungle trails. Edson developed the concept of the "fire team" to spring any traps laid for him. Specially trained, one unit of the team would build up a "base of fire" the moment the force ran into an ambush; then other elements would quickly move out to turn the enemy's flanks.

The link-up between the Coco Patrol and the 11th Regiment's patrols not only protected the mines that bandits had been raiding but reduced the guerrilla activity almost to zero. At least the country was quiet enough, by November of 1928, to hold the presidential election. An American electoral commission headed by General Frank R. McCoy and staffed by specially trained Marines supervised the voting. General Moncada, the candidate of the Liberals, won by a 20,000-vote majority over Adolfo Benard, the Conservatives' candidate. On November 5, two days after the election, *El Commercio,* the chief Liberal organ in the capital, proclaimed in its banner line: "The United States is Vindicated Before the World."

Not entirely, perhaps; but the United States did keep its promise to end the intervention as soon as it seemed feasible. The Marine contingent was gradually reduced as the Guardia was trained by American officers to take over the job of maintaining order. The 11th Marine Regiment, however, stayed at its posts in northern Nicaragua until March, 1931. The reason for its continued presence was the still intransigent Sandino. Even after the Liberal victory at the polls, he stayed in the hills and maintained his disloyal opposition. Financed from the outside, he had "begun to carry on radical propaganda in the interior," as Dana Gardner Munro has written, having veered leftward of both legal political parties.

Sandino stayed on the run until 1933, when a peace agreement was worked out by Dr. Sacasa, who had succeeded to the presidency. Several months later, Sandino was engaged in disarmament talks at Managua with Sacasa and Anastasio Somoza, who was the commander of the Guardia at that time. While Sandino dined with Sacasa's family and a few other guests on the night of February 21, 1934, members of the Guardia, outraged by the leniency granted him under Sacasa's amnesty, and perhaps encouraged by the American minister, Arthur Bliss Lane, agreed that the time had come to kill Sandino. Group responsibility was assured by singing a pact that they called "The Death of Caesar." When Sacasa's congenial group dispersed at about ten o'clock, their automobiles were halted as they emerged from Sacasa's grounds and the Sandinistas among them were whisked off to the Managua airfield to be executed. Somoza himself was conveniently in another part of town and, to the disbelief of the Sandinistas, refused to interpose his authority. A machine gun was positioned, a signal was given, and the prisoners were gunned down. With the Sandinista leadership went the whole movement; its remnants were wiped out within weeks.

Somoza refused to punish those responsible for the assassination. And so the theme of violence, which runs through Nicaraguan political history with the wearying peristence of a Greek tragedy, was sustained. Soon after, Somoza forced Dr. Sacasta to resign, and himself assumed the presidency. Twenty-two years later, still the dictator-president, General Somoza in his turn was assassinated. He has been succeeded in the presidency by his two sons. Early in 1967, Nicaraguan politics again figured in the news, no doubt bemusing veterans of the Marine campaigns of forty years ago who had believed they were bringing the American brand of democracy to that country. Anastasio Somoza, Jr., the younger son, was elected as expected—but only after a flare-up of street fighting in the capital.

The rebellious spirit of Augusto Sandino was not summoned up in any of the news reports of the last election. But it lives on, not only in the mountains where he fought, but as an exemplar throughout the Southern Hemisphere. He was the first to defy the armed power of the Yankee Colossus, and to show that such defiance could be relatively successful if conducted on sound guerrilla principles. Furthermore, his revolution within a revolution, tiny in geographic scope, demonstrated to all who feel that the United States is too quick to intervene in the affairs of its southern neighbors that the American hegemony is maintained by force. The lessons of his rebellion continue to the studied, if not in the U.S. staff colleges, then in the bush camps of Colombia, Venezuela, and other disaffected areas where guerrillas still fight.

Goodbye to the Interurban

William D. Middleton

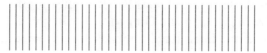

The electric cars dusted along beside dirt roads, sped through the meadows, and brought you right into Main Street. Some were little pinch-waisted wooden affairs, like the Massachusetts car at left, and some were enormous, like the one below, a relic of an unfulfilled dream called the Chicago-New York Air Line. This is an account of how, in a few brief years of glory, the interurban laced America's small towns together with a network of cheap steel rails and copper wire. The automobile, of course, brought all this to an end. Yet today the traffic is so bad that a new kind of interurban is coming back to life.

"Profits almost beyond calculation" prospective stockholders were promised in a series of full-page ads in Chicago newspapers one Sunday in July of 1906. Thus was launched the Chicago-New York Air Line Railroad, and interurban electric railway that would follow a straight line as nearly as was possible, said its promoters, and would whisk passengers between the two cities aboard 100-mile-per-hour trains in just ten hours, cutting eight hours off the fastest steam-train time. The Air Line was the most ambitious interurban project of them all in what, in retrospect, has been described as an ear of "reckless promotion."

In all of America's transportation history there has been nothing quite like the electric interurban. An outgrowth of the urban trolley car, it first appeared only a few years before the end of the nineteenth century, and in barely two booming decades grew to a vast network reaching almost every part of the United States—and then vanished, for all practical purposes, less than half a century after it appeared.

Inventors were trying to develop electric transportation as early as 1834, when a Vermont blacksmith named Thomas Davenport operated a toy electric motor on a miniature railway. But not until 1888, when a youthful inventor named Frank J. Sprague built a twelve-mile streetcar system in Richmond, Virginia, did the electric railway really work on a large trolly system. It was quickly followed by wholesale electrification of America's horse- and cable-car lines.

A United States congressman, Charles L. Henry of Indiana, coined the word "interurban" to describe the two-mile electric line he opened in the spring of 1892 between Anderson and North Anderson, Indiana, but the fifteen-mile East Side Railway, which began operation between Portland and Oregon City, Oregon, in February of 1893, is usually regarded as the first true interurban. Others soon appeared in almost every part of the United States, and by the turn of the century the boom was on.

It seemed to be just what America was waiting for. Local intercity service on the steam railroads was usually slow and infrequent, and the Model T and paved highways were still a few decades away. Frequent service was easy to provide on the interurban, for one car made a train. Fares were almost always lower than steam-road rates. Convenience was still another important factor, for the interurbans stopped almost anywhere, and usually operated into the heart of town over city streets, something that was to doom them in later years.

Travel by interurban was an experience virtually impossible to duplicate today. An infinitely more impressive and elegant vehicle than the city streetcar from which it grew, the interurban car was an imposing sight as it worried its way through the traffic of city streets, bound for the countryside and its own private rails. Once free of the city the big cars sped along at exhilarating speeds, swaying and nosing from side to side on the often uneven track. Windows flung open against the warmth of the summer's day caught the right odors of the countryside, sometimes mingled with the ozone smell generated by the electric traction motors or the pungent odor of grinding brake shoes as the car slowed for a stop. There was a high-pitched screaming from the traction motors and gears, and periodically the air compressor beneath the car cut in with its characteristic *lung-a-lung-a-lung*. The conductor's signal cord, suspended from the ceiling, flip-flopped back and forth, and there was a muffled cracking from the car's ornate woodwork.

A hissing sound from the overhead trolley wire and the rising clatter of its wheels over rail joints signalled the approach of the interurban, and a wailing air horn brought cross traffic to an abrupt halt at a respectful distance from the track. A massive arc headlight and a wooden cowcatcher of imposing size gave the onrushing interurban a commanding presence. Trackside vegetation bent aside in the breeze, and dust clouds rose from road crossings as the electric car sped by in varnished, Gothic-windowed majesty. At night, particularly when the overhead wire was coated with sleet, the countryside was illuminated with great blue flashes every time the racing trolley wheel, or shoe, momentarily lost contact with the wire.

Inside the car, passengers reclined in roomy, plush- or leather-upholstered ease. Carpeted floors were common in some of the more elegant cars, and, on the longer runs, travelers were sometimes treated to buffet-parlor cars, fitted with wicker lounge chairs and equipped with small kitchens from which à la carte meals were served. A few of the longer lines even provided sleeping-car service.

There was an easy informality about interurban travel. Most of the train crews knew their regular clientele on a first-name basis, and they were not above such homely tasks as running a few errands for a housewife along the line, or making a special stop and seeing to the safe arrival of an unescorted child at his destination. The baggage compartment up front was usually piled high with a mélange of express parcels, milk cans, crated baby chicks, and mail bags. On a few of the more important runs the cars even boasted a full-fledged Railway Post Office compartment.

In the earlier years the two-man crew was almost universal. The blue-uniformed, brass-buttoned conductor collected fares, chatted with the passengers, and in the wintertime—if the car wasn't equipped with electric heaters—stoked the coal stove that kept the interior comfortably overheated. Meanwhile the motorman, sealed off in his special compartment, busied himself with the electric controller, air brakes, and air horn. The title "motorman" was almost universal on the interurbans, but a few lines favored the steam roads' more pretentious "engineer." One line, the Puget Sound Electric, couldn't make up its mind which to use and finally compromised on "motoneer." In later years, as an economy move, many lines adopted cars that could be operated by a single man.

Usually interurban lines were quickly and cheaply built. The industry grew prodigiously, if not always wisely. Glib promoters and prideful local boosters, with little regard for traffic potential, brought many lines into being where scarcely a chance for success existed. Big-city street-railway companies and electric utilities frequently went into the interurban business, and such giant enterprises as the Milwaukee Electric Railway & Light Company provided not only electric power and local streetcar lines but also fast interurban service over large areas. In some parts of the United States, principally in New England and the Far West, steam railroads developed extensive interurban systems that acted as freight and passenger feeder-lines to the parent road.

But far more often steam railroads and the inter-urban were bitter rivals, for the electric cars cut heavily into local travel on the steam trains, and sometimes even made a dent in their light-freight and express revenues. Every possible obstacle was usually placed in the way of electric-line construction, and many an interurban, unable to obtain a grade crossing with a steam line, was forced to construct an expensive overpass or underpass. On a few occasions things got rough. Late in 1906, rival construction forces of the Norther Electric Railway and George Gould's Western Pacific, both building toward Sacramento, arrived in Marysville, California, at about the same time. The two routes crossed at a point just south of the Yuba River, where an apiary was located. The Western Pacific men got their rails down first, but the interurban's track gang arrived soon after, and on January 12, 1907, the famous "Battle of the Bee Farm" took place when a hundred Northern Electric men tore out all of the newly laid Western Pacific rails and put down their own. Once the electric cars were running, the steam roads often tried to beat them at their own game, setting up equally frequent schedules at cut-rate fares. Such tactics proved costly and futile, and were usually soon abandoned.

By 1917, when the construction boom had pretty well subsided, there were over 18,000 miles of interurban trackage in the United States and almost 10,000 cars were in operation. Many of the southern, south-western, and mountain states had only a few miles of track, but few were entirely without any. The interurban achieved its greatest growth in five midwestern states: Ohio, Indiana, Michigan, Illinois, and Wisconsin; more than forty per cent of the nation's because of the flatness of the landscape, which cut down construction costs. In Ohio and Indiana the traction network reached almost every city and town of any consequence. There was said to be an interurban line wrapped around nearly every Indiana county courthouse. Indianapolis was America's greatest traction center, with hundreds of miles of track radiating outward in a dozen directions. During 1914, seven million passengers arrived in Indianapolis' Traction Terminal; 520 passenger cars and nearly 100 freight cars departed daily.

The greatest of all America's traction systems was the Pacific Electric Railway, which radiated in every direction from Los Angeles with over 1,000 miles of lines, and reached over 125 cities and communities in southern California. Pacific Electric was largely the work of Henry E. Huntington, wealthy nephew of Collis P. Huntington, one of the Southern Pacific's "Big Four," who acquired a pioneer Los Angeles-Pasadena electric line in 1901 and, in little over a decade, built it into a giant.

Many of Pacific Electric's interurban routes were conceived for purposes of real-estate promotion, and Huntington's profits from his Pacific Electric Land Company were probably at least as great as those earned by his electric cars. Much of southern California grew up along Pacific Electric lines, and such now-populous and prominent areas as Hollywood, Beverly Hills, and the San Fernando Valley were little more than open fields until the "big red cars" arrived.

But the grandest, most intriguing interurban scheme of them all was the Chicago-New York Air Line. Its promoters proposed to build a 750-mile, double-track "super railroad" between that two cities that would be fully 160 miles shorter than any steam route, with running times "10 hours quicker than the quickest" and fares "$10 cheaper than the cheapest." Captivated by the enthusiasm of the line's founder and president, Alexander C. Miller, thousands rushed to buy stock.

As the tracks inched across northern Indian, the stockholders' interest and enthusiasm were bolstered by a monthly newspaper, the *Air Line News,* which trumpeted even the smallest progress as a major achievement, and by such booster organizations as the Kankakee Air Line Stockholders' Association of the World. But Miller's impossibly high construction standards created prohibitive costs, and progress was disappointingly slow. Four years were spent constructing a tremendous fill, nearly two miles long and 290 feet wide at the base, across Coffey Creek Bottoms, east of Gary, Indiana. The might mound of earth was finally completed, but it helped empty the Air Line treasury and exhausted the stockholders' patience. With less than thirty miles of its arrow-straight track built, and only one pair of glossy interurban cars (lettered "Chicago" at one end and "New York" at the other) to show for its promoters' efforts, the Air Line wound up as part of just another small system.

Interurban men, as a rule, refrained from the sort of "public be damned" shenanigans practiced by the steam-railroad barons of earlier days. There were occasional lapses, however. In 1924 Valentine Winters, manager of the Dayton & Western Traction Company, became involved in a squabble with the officials of New Lebanon, Ohio, over paving between the rails which traversed city streets. Unable to reach a satisfactory agreement, Winters disdainfully ripped them up and built a new line around New Lebanon on private right of way. "New Lebanon says Winters is bluffing," headlined a Dayton newspaper at the height of the controversy, which may have had something to do with the name "Valley Bluff" which Winters gave the new station just outside town.

Traction lines were normally constructed in the hope of making a profit for the stockholders, but there were several devoted to more lofty objectives. The Winona Interurban Railway, in Indiana, was constructed by the Winona Assembly and Summer School Session, and its profits went to the operation of a trade school for poor children. When a Tulsa, Oklahoma, oilman established the Sand Springs Home to care for orphans and for widows with children, he endowed it liberally with tracts of industrial land and a multitude of business enterprises, chief among them an interurban, the Sand Springs Railway, which carried passengers until 1954.

Almost from the beginning, interurban proprietors were alert for new methods of attracting extra revenue. Amusement parks were one of the most common traffic builders, and many a company had an "Electric Park" or its equivalent located along its route. When the Stark Electric Railroad was built in northern Ohio soon after the turn of the century, an elaborate park was included in the construction plans. A pond that was dammed to provide water for the line's powerhouse was also stocked with fish, and a large fleet of rowboats was purchased for rental. Playground equipment and picnic facilities were installed on the edge of the pond, and a dance pavilion was erected. Skating on the pond built up winter traffic on the cars.

Pacific Electric operated the world's largest bath house and salt-water plunge at Redondo Beach, California, and an auto race track, the Motordrome, near Playa del Rey. But its greatest tourist attraction was the famed Mount Lowe line, originally built in 1893 by Professor Thaddeus S. D. Lowe, the Civil War balloonist. Interurban cars carried excursionists from Los Angeles up Rubio Canyon, north of Pasadena, to a hotel, dance hall, and refreshment stand. Above Rubio the Great Cable Incline carried them to the summit of Echo Mountain, and there two additional hotels, the Chalet and Echo Mountain House, were surrounded by such attractions as hiking trails and bridle paths, a zoo, a museum, and an observatory equipped with a sixteen-inch telescope. The three-million-candlepower Great World's Fair Searchlight, which Professor Lowe bought and installed on Echo Mountain in 1984, was visible 150 miles at sea.

Above Echo Mountain a narrow-gauge "Alpine Division" carried the excursionists through spectacular mountain scenery to Mount Lowe Springs, when a fourth hotel, the Alpine Tavern, was built 1,100 feet below the summit of the mountain. The narrow-gauge track would through 127 curves in four miles, and crossed eighteen trestles, one of which described an almost complete circle. The roadbed was carved out of solid granite throughout its entire length.

Widely advertised as "the Greatest Mountain Trolley Trip in the World," the Mount Lowe line operated for over forty years, but troubles plagued it from the start. Fire destroyed Echo Mountain House in 1900, and in 1905 a windstorm toppled the Chalet and started a fire that destroyed every building on Echo Mountain but the observatory. A landslide smashed Rubio Hotel to the canyon floor in 1909, and in 1936 a fire wiped out the last hotel. Two years later a cloudburst destroyed most of the railway itself.

A number of midwestern interurbans constructed baseball parks to stimulate traffic, and several Ohio lines organized leagues among communities along their lines. The Cleveland & Southwestern Baseball Trolley League included six towns reached by the interurban; the railway donated a silver cup to the winning team, assisted in advertising the games, and offered free rides to the players. One of the line's officials acted as president of the league.

Various kinds of "theatre specials" were always popular on the interurbans. During the twenties the Chicago, North Shore & Milwaukee operated Grand Opera Specials during the opera season and served a light supper on the return trip. As recently as the mid-fifties it still operated special excursion trains to the chicago Symphony Orchestra's concerts at Ravinia Park, north of Evanston. Nowadays, one inches home hungry through the traffic.

Special trains were often operated for company picnics, loge outings, and similar excursions of the celluloid-collar set, and almost every interurban line of any consequence maintained one or more ornate parlor cars for charter service. As an early test on the operation of electric railways observed, "The chartered car appeals to the feelings of exclusiveness, sense of ownership and comfort beloved of most humans."

Travel over really great distances never amounted to much, but some rather lengthy interurban trips were possible. One could ride from Shawmut, a little town just north of Waterville, Maine, along a series of connecting lines to New York City and then, after crossing the Hudson River by ferry, continue on as far south as Delaware City, Delaware, or as far west as Newville, Pennsylvania. A 1903 article in *World's Work*, which praised the benefits of the "trolly vacation," outlines a trip from Boston to New York that required two days of "hard and steady electric travel" and cost $3.28 in fares. Trolley travel between the two cities became a little less arduous and expensive a few years later when the Old Colony Street Railway Company joined in an overnight trolley-steamer service. Travellers boarded the cars at Post Office Square in Boston for the trip to Fall River, where they transferred to steamers for the overnight run to New York. The cost of that entire trip, a comfortable one, was only $1.75. (Present cost, by railroad, one way, is $11.58; by air, $16, not counting travel to airports; in turnpike tolls alone, $3.30.)

In 1915 the *Interurban Trolley Guide* outlined for the "enthusiastic trolly tourist" a Chicago-to-New York trip which could then be made entirely on interurban lines with the exception of two short stretches in New York State, where it was necessary to use steam trains. The journey took anywhere from thirty-one to forty-five hours, depending on connections, cost about twenty-one dollars, and covered twenty-five different electric railways. Needless to say, the arrangement never caused undue concern on the part of competing steam-railway officials.

One of the first efforts by the trolley people to invade the steam roads' long-haul, luxury market came in 1905, when three electric lines joined in the operation of the deluxe Interstate Limited between Indianapolis and Dayton. The special cars were luxuriously appointed, and a buffet between the two usual compartments—the smoker and the "ladies' parlor"—served light meals from a menu said to be every bit the equal of those on pullman buffet cars.

Sleeping-car service was soon afterward commenced by the Illinois Traction lines, on the 172-mile main line from St. Louis to Peoria. In a time before air conditioning, cinder-free sleepers had distinct advantages over steam-railroad Pullmans. Illinois Traction's berths were fully six inches longer, and its cars were twenty years ahead of Pullman's in providing windows for upper-berth passengers, Every berth had a plush-lined safe-deposit box, and porters served free coffee and rolls in the morning. Only two other lines ever followed Illinois Traction's lead.

Speed was always a matter of concern with electric-railway men. Even though many interurban cars were capable of whisking along at well over sixty miles per hour, over-all running times were anything but rapid during the early years, for tracks were rarely up to it and almost every line had to pass through the streets of cities and towns. As late as 1906 three Ohio inter-urbans were claiming the "fastest electric service in the world," but even their "limiteds" averaged only about thirty-two miles per hour. In local service, they could easily outpace their steam competitors, but when the interurbans made their bid for the long-haul trade, they were at first at a disadvantage.

Many lines stood by conventional car designs, and produced big, powerful steel cars capable of very high speeds. On his three Chicago interurbans, the mid-western utilities magnate Samuel Insull not only introduced handsome new steel cars but spent millions reconstructing and relocating tracks. "Did you ever travel 80 miles an hour?" challenged North Shore Line ads, and all the Insull interurbans enjoyed their most profitable years during the 1920's

Unlike Insull, many traction operators could not afford to reconstruct their roadbeds, and the quest for speed therefore concentrated on new designs for a fast, light car that could operate smoothly over rough track. In 1929 Dr. Thomas Conway, Jr., led a group of investors who assembled the Cincinnati & Lake Erie Railroad from several failing properties, and immediately ordered twenty radical, high-speed interurban cars in an effort to win back the system's declining traffic. They made wide use of aluminum and were equipped with the most powerful motors ever installed in cars of comparable size and weight. They were capable of speeds in excess of ninety miles per hour; in the extensive publicity that surrounded their introduction in 1930, one of them was raced against—and ostensibly defeated—an airplane.

The same year Dr. Conway acquired control of another interurban, the Philadelphia & Western, which was also badly in need of new equipment. The Conway management, setting out to construct an even better car than their Cincinnati & Lake Erie lightweight, launched an intensive research program. In a wind tunnel at the University of Michigan, Professor Felix W. Pawlowski determined that a streamlined car body could be constructed which at speeds over sixty miles per hour would save forty per cent or more of the energy required to move conventional equipment. The ten all-aluminum Bullet cars which were the result of this study could made ninety-two miles per hour.

Almost every interurban was built with an eye toward the passenger trade, but most of them found freight traffic a profitable sideline. Steep grades and the sharp curves common in city streets ruled out the use of standard freight cars on many of the lines, and the interurbans designed and built their own cars for hauling freight cars on many of the lines, and the interurbans designed and built their own cars for hauling light freight. The service was fast, especially by modern standards, and Indiana interurban people boasted that they could deliver shipments anywhere within seventy-five miles of Indianapolis on the same day the goods were ordered. In 1902 interurban lines took in about two million dollars for hauling such commodities as newspapers, mail, milk, and express. By 1922, their freight operations were bringing in forty-five million dollars a year. Interurbans were "piggybacking" truck trailers on flatcars years before the steam railroads enthusiastically adopted the idea. Insull's North Shore Line was the pioneer, in 1926.

No one realized it at the time, of course, but the interurban was doomed almost from the beginning. The villain was the automobile, which had already been invented before the interurban's heyday. Few traction men took it seriously at first; and a few interurbans even found a source of extra revenue in the automobile. In 1905 the general superintendent of the Lake Shore Electric Railway, noting the frequency with which farmers were hauling in disabled cars from the highway that paralleled the railway all the way from Cleveland to Toledo, established an "automobile ambulance" service. It employed a specially equipped flatcar drawn by a freight locomotive. The service, which cost fifteen dollars and up, was said to be "much less embarrassing than having to resort to the horse to get back to town." For a few years around the end of the twenties the Pacific Northwest Traction Company did a lively business hauling trucks, buses, and automobiles around gaps in the uncompleted Pacific Highway north of Seattle.

But gradually the auto began to win out. A few of the weaker interurbans failed soon after World War I, and by the end of the twenties the whole traction network was beginning to crumble as hard-surfaced highways and mass-produced cars spread across the land. Bold, depression-induced interurban consolidations such as the Indiana Railroad System and Ohio's Cincinnati & Lake Erie served only to delay the inevitable; both were gone by World War II. A few lines survived into the war years and enjoyed a brief revival of the bonanza traffic they had once known. Henry Huntington's vast Pacific Electric network, for example, which went into the war virtually intact, handled more passengers in 1945 (109 million of them) than at any other time in its history. But by 1961 the last of its many passenger routes had switched to buses.

The earliest interurban of all, the Portland-Oregon City line, came close to being the last; it survived until early in 1958, having served the Willamette Valley for sixty-five years. Samuel Insull's Chicago lines had become commuter carriers of major importance, but once the wartime traffic had ceased and new roads and freeways made commuting by private automobile as fast as taking the interurbans, the Chicago, Aurora & Elgin and the North Shore line folded up. Of the three Insull interurbans, only the South Shore line continued in operation. The line loses over $500,000 a year on its passenger business, but freight-hauling is so profitable that it offsets the loss. Now major railroads are making efforts to buy control of the South Shore, and once this is accomplished, there will almost certainly be attempts to cut down, and then eliminate, passenger service; the road will probably end up as a dieselized branch of a larger railroad line.

The only other commercial interurban line in Canada or the United States is operated between Upper Darby and Norristown, Pennsylvania, by the Philadelphia Suburban Transportation Company. Recently it purchased two high-speed, streamlined, four-section articulated interurban trains from the defunct Chicago North Shore line and placed them in rush-hour service to supplement Dr. Conway's wind-tunnel-designed Bullet cars, which are now showing their age. The new trains contain a vanishing amenity, a bar-lounge section for suburban commuters. How long this service will last is problematical, especially in view of the impending takeover of the line by a transit authority. Authorities and amenities rarely go together.

The interurban may be nearly gone, but it will not soon be forgotten. Once it was evident that the few remaining lines were disappearing and their cars and other equipment were headed for the scrap heap, a new fraternity arose—trolly-museum enthusiasts, who now number in the thousands. Several museum groups have been formed for the sole purpose of saving representative interurban cars by purchasing them at scrap prices, buying an abandoned right of way, and putting the cars in service again for the entertainment of children who have never ridden an interurban and of their elders in whom nostalgia runs strong.

A dozen such lines are now in service, and more are in the planning stage. The largest, and the first to be formed, is located at Kennebunkport, Maine, where the right of way of a defunct interurban line was purchased all the way to Biddeford, six miles to the north. Although only a mile of track is now in operation, more than eighty trolleys and interurban cars have been acquired, and the line, the Seashore Electric Railway, can eventually build its track right into the streets of Biddeford. Similar lines run at Branford and Warehouse Point, Connecticut, with cars of many varieties.

The real interurban is gone—yet not quite. The highways and freeways that doomed so many interurban lines—simply because it was much cheaper to run a bus over someone else's roads than to build a railroad with expensive poles and overhead wire—are now so overburdened that in rush hours traffic stagnates. The answer in all urban areas now is clearly rapid transit, the electrically operated rail line that can whisk riders into and out of cities without the long rush-hour delays.

Consider, for instance, Louisville, Kentucky, where sixty-five years ago a rapid-transit system was developed at considerable cost. It took riders from suburban areas into downtown Louisville along seven different routes by interurban lines of the Louisville & Interurban Railroad. Then the automobile and bus came along, and the competition was too much. The interurban lines gave up and were dismantled. The rights of way were sold. Today city planners in Louisville, as in San Francisco, Washington, and most other swollen urban complexes, are planning vast expenditures for rapid-transit lines. What routes will they take? You guessed it: much the same as the interurbans of the past. As Louisville's city works director says, "I think we're coming around full-cycle on this thing. It's a shame that the old interurban lines didn't survive."

The big old electric car, dusting through the meadows with its air horn shrieking for the crossings, is only a museum piece. Yet something is coming back, something without the wicker and the inlaid woodwork, something a little too streamlined and shiny perhaps, but something to hearten those who loved the most open road of all, the rails of the interurban.

Who Started the Cold War?

Charles L. Mee, Jr.

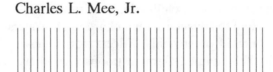

The Cold War—we have spent a generation hearing abnout it, thinking about it, worrying about it. We all know it somehow grew out of World War II, that it involved conflict between the United States and the Soviet Union, and that it led to a series of frightining confrontations: the Berlin airlift; the escalating stages of the nuclear arms race; the Cuban missile crisis; the wars in Korea and Vietnam. But what really *caused* the Cold War? It is not a simple question, and knowledgeable and honest men can differ considerably in answering it.

On the following pages, Charles L. Mee, Jr., formerly editor of HORIZON magazine and the author of *Meeting at Potsdam* (1975) and, currently, *A Visit to Haldeman and Other States of Mind,* presents an unorthodox view of how the Cold War began. He is replied to by W. Averell Harriman, former U.N. ambassador to the Soviet Union and a distinguished participant in some of the relevant events, writing in collaboraiton with Elie Abel, dean of the Columbia University School of Journalism; finally Mr. Mee is given space for a brief rebuttal. It all adds up, we think, to a most thoughtful and provocative consideration of an awesome fact of the modern world that has overshadowed our lvies and our childrens' lives, and will continue to do so.

On April 12, 1945, Franklin Roosevelt died, and soon afterward Vyascheslav M. Molotov, the Russian foreign minister, stopped by in Washington to pay his respects to Harry Truman, the new President. Truman received Molotov in the oval Office and, as Truman recalled it, chewed him out "bluntly" for the way the Russians were behaving in Poland. Molotov was stunned. He had never, he told Truman, "been talked to like that in my life."

"Carry out your agreements," Truman responded, "and you won't get talked to like that."

That's a good way to talk, if you want to start an argument. . . .

In Europe, Germany surrendered to the Allies on May 8. On May 12, Prime Minister Winston Churchill sent Truman an ominous cable about the Russians: "An iron curtain is drawn down upon their front," Churchill said, and, moreover, "it would be open to the Russians in a very short time to advance if they chose to the waters of the north Sea and Atlantic." On May 17, Churchill ordered his officers not to destroy any German planes. In fact, Churchill kept 700,000 captured German troops in military readiness, prepared to be turned against the Russians.

That, too, is a good way to behave, if you are looking for trouble. . . .

Joseph Stalin said little: he did not advance his troops to the Atlantic, but he planted them firmly throughout eastern Europe and, in violation of previous agreements with the British and Americans, systematically crushed all vestiges of democratic government in Poland, Hungary, Czechoslovakia, Bulgaria, Rumania, Yugoslavia, and Finland. In truth, not quite: the Finns had managed to salvage a few bits and scraps of democratic usage for themselves. At dinner one night in the Kremlin, Andrei Zhdanov, one of Stalin's propagandists, complained that the Russians should have occupied Finland. "Akh, Finland," said Molotov, "that is a peanut."

And that, too, is a nice way to behave, if you are trying to stir up a fight. . . .

Most people, most of the time want peace in the world, and they imagine that most politicians, being human, share the same wishes. At the end of a war, presumably, the desire for peace is most intense and most widely shared. Lamentably, that is not always the case. At the end of World War II the Russians, as Churchill remarked, feared "our friendship more than our enmity."

The Russians had both immediate cause and long-standing historical reasons for anxiety.

"From the beginning of the ninth century," as Louis Halle, a former State Department historian, has written, "and even today, the prime driving force in Russian has been fear. . . . The Russians as we know them today have experienced ten centuries of constant, mortal fear. This has not been a disarming experience. It has not been an experience calculated to produce a simple, open, innocent, and guileless society." Scattered over a vast land with no natural frontiers for protection, as Halle remarks, the Russians have been overrun "generation after generation, by fresh waves of invaders. . . . Lying defenseless on the plain, they were slaughtered and subjugated and humiliated by the invaders time and again."

Thus the Russians sought to secure their borders along eastern Europe. The czars attempted this, time and again: to secure a buffer zone, on their European frontier, a zone that would run down along a line that would later be called the Iron Curtain.

Yet, at the end of World War II, Stalin's fears were not just fears of outsiders. World War II had shown that his dictatorship was not only brutal but also brutally inept; he was neither a great military leader nor a good administrator; and the Russian soldiers returning from the Western Front had seen much evidence of Western prosperity. Stalin needed the Cold War, not to venture out into the world again after an exhausting war, but to discipline his restless people at home. He had need of that ancient stratagem of monarchs—the threat of an implacable external enemy to be used to unite his own people in Russia.

Churchill, on the other hand, emerged from World War II with a ruined empire irretrievably in debt, an empire losing its colonies and headed inevitably toward bankruptcy. Churchill's scheme for saving Great Britain was suitably inspired and grand: he would, in effect, reinvent the British Empire; he would establish an economic union of Europe (much like what the Common Market actually became); this union would certainly not be led by vanquished Germany or Italy, not by so small a power as the Netherlands, not by devastated France, but by Great Britain. To accomplish this aim, unfortunately, Churchill had almost nothing in the way of genuine economic or military power left; he had only his own force of persuasion and rhetoric. He would try to parlay those gifts into American backing for England's move into Europe. The way to bring about American backing was for Churchill to arrange to have America and Russia quarrel; while America and Russia quarreled, England would—as American diplomats delicately put it—"lead" Europe.

Truman, for his part, led a nation that was strong and getting stronger. Henry Luce, the publisher of the influential *Time* and *Life* magazines, declared that this was to be the beginning of "the American Century"—and such a moment is rarely one in which a national leader wants to maintain a status quo. The United States was securing the Western Hemisphere, moving forcefully into England's collapsing "sterling bloc," acquiring military and economic positions over an area of the planet so extensive that the sun could never set on it.

The promise was extraordinary, the threat equally so. The United States did not practice Keynesian economics during the 1930's. It was not Roosevelt's New Deal that ran up the enormous federal deficit or built the huge, wheezing federal bureaucracy of today. War ran up the deficit; war licked the depression; war made the big federal government. In 1939, after a decade of depression, after the Civilian Conservation Corps, the Public Works Administration, the Civil Works Administration, the Agricultural Adjustment Act, the Social Security Act, and all the rest of the New Deal efforts on behalf of social justice, the federal budget was $9 billion. In 1945 it was $100 billion.

American prosperity was built upon deficit spending for war. President Truman knew it, and maintained deficit spending with the Cold War. Eventually, with the Truman Doctrine and the Marshall Plan, the encouragement of American multinational companies, and a set of defense treaties that came finally to encompass the world, he institutionalized it. The American people might find this easier to damn if they had not enjoyed the uncommon prosperity it brought them.

In October, 1944, Churchill visited Stalin in Moscow. The need then, clearly, was for cooperation among the Allies in order to win the war—and it appeared at the time that the cooperativeness nurtured during the war could be continued afterward. Each had only to recognize the other's vital interests. Churchill commenced to outline those interests to be recognized for the sake of the post war cooperation.

"I said," Churchill recalled, " 'Let us settle about our affairs in the Balkans. Your armies are in Rumania and Bulgaria. We have interests, missions, and agents there. Don't let us get at cross-purposes in small ways. So far as Britain and Russia are concerned, how would it do for you to have ninety per cent predominance in Rumania, for us to have ninety per cent of the say in Greece, and go fifty-fifty about Yugoslavia?' "

Churchill wrote this out on a piece of paper, noting, too, a split of Bulgaria that gave Russia 75 per cent interest, and a fifty-fifty split of Hungary. He pushed the piece of paper across the table to Stalin, who placed a check mark on it and handed it back. There was a silence. "At length I said, 'Might it not be thought rather cynical if it seemed we had disposed of these issues, so fateful to millions of people, in such an offhand manner? Let us burn the paper.' 'No, you keep it.' said Stalin."

Such casual and roughshod "agreements" could hardly be the last word on the matter; yet, they signified a mutual recognition of one another's essential interests and a willingness to accommodate one another's needs—while, to be sure, the smaller powers were sold out by all sides. At this same time, in October, 1944, and later on in January, 1945, Roosevelt entered into armistice agreements with Britain and Russia that gave Stalin almost complete control of the internal affairs of the ex-Nazi satellites in eastern Europe. As a briefing paper that the State Department prepared in the spring of 1945 for President Truman said, "spheres of influence do in fact exist," and "eastern Europe is, in fact, a Soviet sphere of influence."

In short, the stage was set for postwar peace: spheres of influence had been recognized; a tradition of negotiation had been established. Yet, the European phase of World War II was no sooner ended than symptoms of the Cold War began to appear. The Big Three no longer needed on another to help in the fight against Hitler, and the atomic bomb would soon settle the war against Japan.

Toward the end of May, 1945, Harry Hopkins arrived in Moscow to talk with Stalin, to feel out the Russians now that the war in Europe had ended, and to prepare the agenda for discussion at the Potsdam Conference that would be held in Germany in mid-July. The United States had a problem, Hopkins informed Stalin, a problem so serious that it threatened "to affect adversely the relations between our two countries." The problem was, Hopkins said, Poland: "our inability to carry into effect the Yalta Agreement on Poland."

But, what was the problem? Stalin wanted to know. A government had been established there, under the auspices of the occupying Red Army, a government that was, naturally, "friendly" to the Soviet Union. there could be no problem—unless others did not wish to allow the Soviet Union to ensure a friendly government in Poland.

"Mr. Hopkins stated," according to the notes taken by his interpreter, Charles Bohlen, "that the United States would desire a Poland friendly to the Soviet Union and in fact desired to see friendly countries all along the Soviet borders.

"Marshal Stalin replied if that be so we can easily come to terms in regard to Poland."

But, said Hopkins, Stalin must remember the Declaration on Liberated Europe (signed at the Yalta Conference in February, 1945) and its guarantees for democratic governments; here was a serious difference between them; Poland had become the issue over which cooperation between Russia and America would flourish or fail.

Evidently Stalin could not understand this demand; apparently he could not believe that Americans were sincerely so idealistic. Did not America, after all, support a manifestly undemocratic dictatorship in Franco's Spain? "I am afraid," Averell Harriman, the U.S. ambassador to the Soviet Union, cabled home to Truman, "Stalin does not and never will fully understand our interest in a free Poland as a matter of principle. He is a realist in all of his actions, and it is hard for him to appreciate our faith in abstract principles. It is difficult for him to understand why we should want to interfere with Soviet policy in a country like Poland, which he considers so important to Russia's security, unless we have some ulterior motive."

And indeed, Russia's sphere of influence was recognized, it seemed, only so that it might serve as a bone of contention. Poland, Czechoslovakia, Bulgaria, Rumania, Hungary, all became bones of contention. It is not clear that any one of the Big Three deeply cared what happened to these eastern European countries so long as the countries served as useful pawns. Hopkins insisted that Stalin must recognize freedom of speech, assembly, movement, and religious worship in Poland and that all political parties (except fascists) must be "permitted the free use, without distinction, of the press, radio, meetings and other facilities of political expression." Furthermore, all citizens must have "the right of public trial, defense by counsel of their own choosing, and the right of habeas corpus."

Of course, Stalin said, of course, "these principles of democracy are well known and would find no objection on the part of the Soviet Government." To be sure, he said, "in regard to the *specific* [italics added] freedoms mentioned by Mr. Hopkins, they could only be applied in full in peace time, and even then with certain limitations."

In the latter two weeks of July, 1945, the Big Three gathered at Potsdam, just outside of Berlin, for the last of the wartime conferences. They discussed the issues with which the war in Europe had left them, and with which the war in the Far East would leave them when it came to an end. They discussed spheres of influence, the disposition of Germany, the spoils of war, reparations, and, of course, eastern Europe.

At one of the plenary sessions of the Potsdam Conference, they outlined the spheres of influence precisely, clearly, and in detail during a discussion of the issue of "German shares, gold, and assets abroad." To whom did these items belong? What, for instance, did Stalin mean when he said "abroad?"

STALIN: ". . . the Soviet delegation . . . will regard the whole of Western Germany as falling within your sphere, and Eastern Germany, within ours."

Truman asked whether Stalin meant to establish "a line running from the Baltic to the Adriatic." Stalin replied that he did.

STALIN: "As to the German investments, I should put the question this way: as to the German investments in Eastern Europe, they remain with us, and the rest, with you. . . ."

TRUMAN: "Does this apply only to German investments in Europe or in other countries as well?"

STALIN: "Let me put it more specifically: the German investments in Rumania, Bulgaria, Hungary, and Finland go to us, and all the rest to you."

FOREIGN MINISTER ERNEST BEVIN: "The German investments in other countries go to us?"

STALIN: "In all other countries, in South America, in Canada, etc., all this is your. . . ."

SECRETARY OF STATE JAMES BYRNES: "If an enterprise is not in Eastern Europe but in Western Europe or in other parts of the world, that enterprise remains ours?"

STALIN: "In the United States, in Norway, in Switzerland, in Sweden, in Argentina [general laughter], etc.—all that is yours."

A delegation of Poles arrived at Potsdam to argue their own case before the Big Three. The Poles, struggling desperately and vainly for their land, their borders, their freedoms, did not seem to understand that their fate was being settled for reasons that had nothing to do with them. They wandered about Potsdam, trying to impress their wishes on the Big Three. "I'm sick of the bloody Poles," Churchill said when they came to call on him. "I don't want to see them. Why can't Anthony [Eden] talk to them?" Alexander Cadogan, Permanent Undersecretary for Foreign Affairs, found the Poles at Eden's house late one night and "had to entertain them as bets I could, and went on entertaining them— no signs of A. He didn't turn up till 11:30. . . . So then we got down to it, and talked shop till 1:30. Then filled the Poles (and ourselves) with sandwiches and whiskies and sodas and I went to bed at 2 A.M." Altogether, it had been an agreeable enough evening, although in general, Cadogan confided to his diary, he found the Poles to be "dreadful people. . . ."

Germany, too, provided a rich field for contention. The answer to the German question became a simple but ticklish matter of keeping Germany sufficiently weak so that it could not start another war and yet, at the same time, sufficiently strong to serve as a buffer against Russia, or, from Russia's point of view, against the Western powers. To achieve this delicate balance, the Big Three haggled at Potsdam over complex set of agreements about zones of authority, permissible levels of postwar industry, allocation of resources of coal and foodstuffs, spoils of war, reparations, and other matters. The country as a whole was divided into administrative zones in which Allied commanders had absolute veto powers over some matters, and, in other respects, had to defer to a central governmental council for measure to be applied uniformly to Germany.

Out of all these careful negotiations came the astonishing fact that Germany was established as the very center and source of much of the anxiety and conflict of the Cold War. How this could happened is one of the wonders of the history of diplomacy. The discussions and bargaining at Potsdam among Churchill, Truman, and Stalin, and among the foreign ministers, and on lower levels, among economic committees and subcommittees, is maddeningly tangled; but, once all of the nettlesome complexities are cleared away, the postwar arrangement for Germany can be seen with sudden and arresting clarity. The Big Three agreed to have a Germany that would be politically united—but, at the very same time, economically divided. They agreed, then, to create a country that could never be either wholly united nor entirely divided, neither one Germany nor two Germanies, but rather a country that would be perpetually at war with itself, and, since its two halves would have two patrons, would keep its two patrons in continuous conflict. Whether this postwar arrangement for Germany was intentional or inadvertent, it was certainly a diplomatic tour de force. In 1949, with the formation of the West German and East German governments, the contradictions of the Potsdam policy became overt.

Eastern Europe, Germany, and the atomic bomb were the three most striking elements of the early Cold War. It was while he was at the Potsdam Conference that President Truman received news that the test of the bomb at Alamogordo had been successful. By that time the bomb was no longer militarily necessary to end the war against Japan ;the Japanese were near the end and were attempting to negotiate peace by way of their ambassador to Moscow. After the bomb was dropped, Truman would maintain that it had avoided the invasion of the Japanese maintained and so saved a million American lives. But was that true?

General Henry (Hap) Arnold, chief of the Army Air Forces, said before the atomic device was dropped on Japan, that conventional bombing would end the war without an invasion. Admiral Ernest J. King, chief of U.S. naval operations, advised that a naval blockade alone would end the war. General Eisenhower said it was "completely unnecessary" to drop the bomb, and that the weapon was "no longer mandatory as a measure to save American lives." Even General George Marshall, U.S. chief of staff and the strongest advocate at that late hour for the bomb's use, advised that the Japanese at least be forewarned to give them a chance to surrender. Diplomats advised Truman that he need only have Russia sign his proclamation calling for Japanese surrender; the Russians had not yet declared war against Japan, and so the Japanese still had hopes that the Russians would help them negotiate peace; if Russia signed the proclamation, the Japanese would see that their last chance was gone and would surrender. None of this advice was followed.

After the war, the United States Strategic Bombing Command issued a study confirming the advice Truman had been getting before he gave the order to drop the atomic bomb: "Japan would have surrendered even if the atomic bombs had not been dropped, even if Russia had not entered the war, and even if no invasion had been planned or contemplated." Then why was it dropped? Admiral William Leahy, Truman's top aide, was unable to offer the puzzled British chiefs of staff a better explanation than that it was "because of the vast sums that had been spent on the project," although he commented that in using the bomb, the Americans "had adopted an ethical standard common to the barbarians of the Dark Ages."

However that may be, its use must have been chilling to Stalin; doubly chilling if Stalin realized that the United States had used the bomb even when it was not militarily necessary. Indeed, according to Secretary of State James Byrnes, that was the real reason why the bomb was used after all—"to make Russia," as he said, "more manageable in Europe." Perhaps it is because that constituted a war crime—to kill people when it is not militarily necessary is a crime according to international accord—that Truman insisted to his death, and in obstinate defiance of all other opinion, that it was militarily necessary.

The bomb may have been dropped, too, in order to end the war against Japan without Russian help. The Russians had promised to enter the war in the Far East exactly three months after the war in Europe ended—which it did on May 8. Truman's aim was not merely to end the war against Japan, but to end it before August 8.

When word reached Potsdam that the atomic bomb had been successfully tested, Truman was enormously pleased. When the news was passed along to Churchill, the prime minister was overcome with delight at the "vision—fair and bright indeed it seemed—of the end of the whole war in one or two violent shocks." Churchill understood at once that "we should not need the Russians," and he concluded that "we seemed suddenly to have become possessed of a merciful abridgment of the slaughter in the East and of a far happier prospect in Europe. I have not doubt that these thoughts were present in the minds of my American friends."

The problem was what to tell the Russians. Presumably, as allies of the Americans and British, they needed to be told of this new weapon in which Truman and Churchill placed such tremendous hopes. yet, if the Russians were told, they might rush to enter the war against Japan and so share in the victory. "The President and I no longer felt that we needed [Stalin's] aid to conquer Japan," Church wrote. And so Stalin must be told about the existence of the bomb—and at the same time he must not be told. In short, Truman and Churchill decided, Stalin must be informed so casually as not to understand that he was being informed of much of anything.

On July 24, after one of the sessions of the Potsdam Conference, Truman got up from the baize-covered table and sauntered around to Stalin. The President had left his interpreter, Charles Bohlen, behind and relied on Stalin's personal translator—signifying that he had nothing important to say, just idle, end-of-the-day chit-chat.

"I was perhaps five yards away," Churchill recalled, "and I watched with the closest attention the momentous talk. I knew what the President was going to do. What was vital to measure was its effect on Stalin. I can see it all as if it were yesterday."

"I casually mentioned to Stalin," Truman wrote in his memoirs, "that we had new weapon of unusual destructive force. The Russian Premier showed no special interest. All he said was that he was glad to hear it and hoped we would make 'good use of it against the Japanese.' "

"I was sure," Churchill said, "that [Stalin] had no idea of the significance of what he was being told . . . his face remained gay and genial and the talk between these two potentates soon came to an end. As we were waiting for our cars I found myself near Truman. 'How did it go?' I asked. 'He never asked a question,' he replied."

According to the Russian General Shtemenko, the ploy worked: the Russian Army staff "received no special instructions" after this meeting. According the Marshal Georgi K. Zhukov, commander of the Russian zone of occupation in Germany, Stalin returned from the meeting and told Molotov about Truman's remarks. Molotov "reacted immediately: 'Let them. We'll have to talk it over with Kurchatov and get him to speed things up.' I realized they were talking about research on the atomic bomb."

Whatever the case, whether Stalin realized what he had been told at the time, or only in retrospect, the nuclear arms race began, in effect, at Potsdam, on July 24, 1945, at 7:30 P.M.

Distrust, suspicion, anxiety, fear—all were intensified at Potsdam, and to them were added harshness and provocation, from all sides. During the next few months the agreements that had been reached were violated, or used as the bases of accusations of duplicity and bad faith. Many of the questions raised at Potsdam had been postponed and delegated to a Council of Foreign Ministers that was established to deal with these questions, and new ones, as they arose. The first meeting of the council was set for September, 1945. James Byrnes, before he left Washington to attend the meeting, had chatted with Secretary of War Henry Stimson. "I found that Byrnes was very much against any attempt to cooperate with Russia." Stimson noted in his diary. "His mind is full of his problems with the coming meeting of foreign ministers and he looks to have the presence of the bomb in his pocket, so to speak, as a great weapon to get through the thing. . . ." The British Chancellor of the Exchequer, Rt. Hon. Hugh Dalton, asked Foreign Minister Ernest Bevin how things were going, once the meeting started. "Like the strike leader said." Bevin replied, "thank God there is no danger of settlement."

Not everyone was so quick or so eager to encourage the start of the Cold War. Henry Stimson was very much the elder statesman in 1945; he had spent more than fifty years in assorted government positions, and he foresaw dread consequences in Truman's developing policies toward Russia. Stimson had long thought that America should be tough with the Soviet Union, but he now believed that toughness was turning into harshness and harshness into provocativeness. In a memo that he wrote Truman in the autumn of 1945, he focused his thoughts around one of the most vexing problems of the postwar world:

". . . I consider the problem of our satisfactory relations with Russia as not merely of our satisfactory relations with Russia as not merely connected with but as virtually dominated by the problem of the atomic bomb. Except for the problem of the control of that bomb, those relations, while vitally important, might not be immediately pressing. . . . But with the discovery of the bomb, they became immediately emergent. These relations may be perhaps irretrievably embittered by the way in which we approach the solution of the bomb with Russia. For if we fail to approach them now and merely continue to negotiate with them, having this weapon rather ostentatiously on our hip, their suspicions and their distrust of our purposes and motives will increase. . . .

"The chief lesson I have learned in a long life is that the only way you can make a man trustworthy is to trust him; and the surest way to make him untrustworthy is to distrust him and show your distrust."

Men like Stimson—and Henry Wallace, then Secretary of Commerce—were allowed, or forced, to resign. Others, those who tended to believe in an aggressive attitude toward Russia, were spotted, and promoted—young men such as John Foster Dulles and Dean Rusk. George Kennan, then in the American embassy in Moscow, was discovered after he sent a perfervid 8,000-word cable back to Washington: "We have here a political force committed fanatically to the belief that with U.S. there can be no permanent modus vivendi, that it is desirable and necessary that the internal harmony of our society be disrupted, our traditional way of life be destroyed, the international authority of our state be broken. .. ." In his memoirs, kennan says that he now looks back on his cable "with horrified amusement." At the time, however, he was ideal for Truman's use, and he was recalled from Moscow and made chairman of the State Department's Policy Planning Committee, or as the *New York Times* called him, "America's global planner."

At Potsdam, the Big Three had all agreed to remove their troops from Iran. They set a deadline of March 2, 1946, and, as the deadline approached, the British announced that they would be leaving. The Russians, however, let it be known that they were somewhat reluctant to leave until they had made an agreement with the Iranians for an oil concession, and, regardless even of that agreement, Stalin rather thought he would like to withdraw only from central Iran and keep some troops in northern Iran. Not all these matters were immediately clarified and so, on March 1, 1946, Stalin announced that Russian soldiers would remain in Iran "pending clarification of the situation."

President Truman, meanwhile, invited Winston Churchill to deliver an address in March, 1946, at Fulton, Missouri: "A shadow has fallen upon the scenes so lately lighted by the Allied victory," said the former prime minister. "Nobody knows what Soviet Russia and its Communist international organization intends to do in the immediate future, or what are the limits, if any, to their expansive and proselytising tendencies. . . . From Stettin in the Baltic to Trieste in the Adriatic [the line, as Churchill neglected to mention, to which he and Truman had agreed at Potsdam], an iron curtain has descended across the Continent. Behind that line lie all the capitals of the ancient state of Central and Eastern Europe . . . in what I must call the Soviet sphere . . . this is certainly not the Liberated Europe we fought to build up. Nor is it one which contains the essentials of permanent peace."

In Moscow, a well-rehearsed Russian reporter quizzed Stalin.

QUESTION: "How do you appraise Mr. Churchill's latest speech in the United States?"

STALIN: "I appraise it as a dangerous act, calculated to sow the seeds of dissention among the Allied states and impede their collaboration."

QUESTION: "Can it be considered that Mr. Churchill's speech is prejudicial to the cause of peace and security?"

STALIN: "Yes, unquestionably. As a matter of fact, Mr. Churchill not takes the stand of the warmongers, and in this Mr. Churchill is not alone. He has friends not only in Britain but in the United States of American as well."

During the winter of 1946–47, a succession of snowstorms hit Britain. Coal was already in short supply; factories had already closed for lack of fuel that winter. With the blizzards came rationing, first of electricity and then of food; finally heat was cut off. Britain, as Louis Halle wrote, "was like a soldier wounded in war who, now that fighting was over, was bleeding to death." The empire was at last dying.

In Washington, on February 21, 1947, a Friday afternoon, First Secretary H. M. Sichel of the British embassy delivered two notes to Loy Henderson at the State Department. Until that moment, Britain had been the principal support for the economy of Greece and the provider for the Turkish Army. The first of Sichel's notes said that Britain could no longer support Greece; the second said Britain could no longer underwrite the Turkish Army. "What the two notes reported," Halle observed. "was the final end of the *Pax Britannica.*"

The following week, on February 27, Truman met with congressional leaders in the White House. Undersecretary of State Dean Acheson was present at the meeting, and Truman had him tell the congressmen what was at stake. Acheson spoke for ten minutes, informing the legislators that nothing less than the survival of the whole of Western civilization was in the balance at that moment; he worked in references to ancient Athens, Rome, and the course of Western civilization and freedoms since those times. The congressmen were silent for a few moments, and then, at last, Senator Arthur Vandenberg of Michigan, a prominent Republican who had come to support an active foreign policy, spoke up. All this might be true, Vandenberg said; but, if the President wished to sell his program to the American people, he would have to "scare hell out of the country." it was at that moment that the Cold War began in earnest for the United States.

It would be nice to be able to say that one nation held back from the nattering and abusiveness, that one seemed reluctant to start a conflict with its former allies, that one tried to compose the differences that had predictably arisen at the end of the war, that this one was the first to make a provocative move or charge and that one was last—but in truth all three leaped into the fray with such haste and determination that the origins of the Cold War are lost in a blur of all three sides hastening to be first in battle.

It is difficult to know the effects the Cold War had upon the Russian people in these years. But America paid heavy costs. When a nation has an actively internationalist, interventionist foreign policy, political power in that country tends to flow to the central government, and, within the central government, to the executive branch. That there was, in recent times, the creation of an "imperial presidency" in the U.S. was no quirk or happenstance; it was the natural outgrowth of the Cold War. From the imperial presidency, from the disorientation of the constitutional system of checks and balances, Watergate, proteiform and proliferating spy organizations, the impotence and decadence of Congress—all these were almost inevitable. That is why George Washington, a profoundly sophisticated man, advised Americans to avoid foreign entanglements; and that is why Americans who prize their freedom have always been a peace-loving people.

How the Media Seduced and Captured American Politics

Richard C. Wade

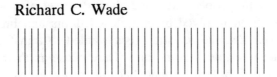

Television has been accused of many things: vulgarizing tastes; trivializing public affairs; sensationalizing news; corrupting the young; pandering to profits; undermining traditional values. The indictments are no doubt too harsh, and they ignore the medium's considerable achievements over two decades. Yet even the severest critics have not noticed the way in which television first seduced and then captured the whole American political process.

The fact is that each year fewer people register to vote, and among those who do, an ever-shrinking number actually go to the polls. Since casting a free ballot constitutes the highest expression of freedom in a democracy, its declining use is a grave matter. How did we get ourselves into this perilous state?

Television's victory was not the result of a carefully planned and calculated assault on our political procedures; less still was it the conspiracy of a greedy and power-hungry industry. Rather it was a process in which each year witnessed a modest expansion of the electronic influence on American politics. A look at the presidential election of 1948, the first of the age of television, suggests both the magnitude and swiftness of the change. President Harry Truman ran a shoestring campaign sustained largely by his incumbency and the overconfidence of his opponent. Together the two candidates spent only about $15 million—the cost of a gubernatorial contest in New York three decades later. Both presidential candidates leaned heavily on their state and local parties for crowds and election-day support. Truman's whistle-stop tour of the country harked back to century-old technique. Television covered the conventions but intruded no further. Radio handled the late returns, and the commentator H. V. Kaltenborn, who assumed historical patterns would hold true, waited for the rural vote to sustain his early prediction of a victory for New York governor Thomas E. Dewey.

Some of the possibilities of television emerged, however, in the next election. Sen. Robert Taft used time-honored, if somewhat questionable, tactics to line up a solid phalanx of Southern delegates at the 1952 Republican convention. Gen. Dwight Eisenhower's managers presented a more properly selected alternative set of delegates. Historically, disputes of this kind had been resolved behind closed doors and brought to the convention only for ratification. But Eisenhower strategists wanted to transform what had long been seen as a technical question into a moral one. They chose as their weapon televised committee hearings. For the first time, public became privy to the vagaries of party rules. Viewers were let into the smoke-filled room. The result was a resounding defeat for Taft, and Eisenhower went into the convention with plenty of delegates and wearing the fresh, smiling face of reform.

A few months later Eisenhower's running mate, Richard Nixon, found himself entangled in a burgeoning scandal involving a private fund raised by large contributors to advance his political career. Though no law had been broken, the impropriety was clear, especially in a campaign based on cleaning up "the mess" in Washington. Eisenhower declared that anyone in public life should be as "clean as a hound's tooth,'" and many of his advisers told him to drop the young congressman.

A desperate Nixon decided to take his case directly to the public—through a half-hour paid telecast. He declared he head meant no wrongdoing, detailed the high costs facing a California congressman, noted his own modest means, and said he had always voted his own conscience on issues before the House. Most memorable, however, was his use of his dog, Checkers, as a kind of surrogate "hound's tooth." To sophisticates it seemed like a clip out of a daytime soap opera, but the public found it plausible enough. More important, it satisfied Dwight Eisenhower.

These two episodes revealed the ambiguity of the new medium. Until 1952, conventions had been closed party affairs run by the national committees. In fact, that is still their only legal function. But television put the voters on the convention floor. Both parties had to dispense with a lot of the traditional hoopla—endless floor demonstrations, marathon seconding speeches, visibly indulgent behavior by delegates—and keynote speakers had to project telegenic appeal as well as party service. To be sure, television introduced its own brand of hoopla. Cameras zoomed in on outrageous costumes, floormen interviewed colorful if not always important figures, and networks did the counting of the delegates before the issues or nominations actually got to the decisive stage.

The Nixon heritage was less complicated. The "Checkers" speech became shorthand for slick, calculated manipulation if not deception. Critics argued it demonstrated that a shrewd master of the medium could sell anything—not only commercial products but political candidates as well.

The presidential election of 1956 was essentially a rerun of the previous one, yet one episode demonstrated the increasing influence of television. With Stevenson's renomination by the Democrats a certainty, the networks faced a four-day yawn from their viewers. Salvation suddenly appeared in a contest over the Vice-Presidency. With no obvious choice and with Stevenson himself undecided, three senators moved into contention: Estes Kefauver of Tennessee, Hubert Humphrey of Minnesota, and John F. Kennedy of Massachusetts.

Chicago was awash with whispers of deals being concocted in smoke-filled rooms to designate a running mate, and to sustain his reform image, Stevenson threw open the choice to the convention. Suddenly there was theater. Kefauver had a second chance; Humphrey got his first; and Kennedy seemed to have no chance at all. A big scoreboard behind to podium recorded the voting from the floor. The Kentucky Derby never generated more excitement. As state by state announced the results, the lead fluctuated. At the last moment Humphrey released his delegates to the Tennessean who had contested Stevenson in a dozen primaries. Afterward only historians would remember that Kefauver had won, but Kennedy's performance gave the public its first impression of a man who would dominate his party—and the media—for almost a decade.

Four years later another national election provided television with one of its greatest moments: the Nixon-Kennedy debates. It was a strange event, and it is hard to say who won. A reading of the transcripts today reveals no surprises. Each candidate expressed views already known; each circled and jabbed; but there were no knockdowns. Yet millions saw the relative newcomer under the most favorable of circumstances, and even though the contrast was sharper visually than intellectually, there was vague general feeling that JFK had got the better of it.

In all, the new medium lived up both to its responsibilities and its possibilities. For the first time, it had brought two presidential candidates to the same podium. The proceedings were overly elaborate, but the handling of the event was scrupulously fair and nonpartisan. And afterward it would become increasingly hard for candidates, even incumbents, to avoid legitimate challenges on television.

The turbulence of the sixties can only be understood in the context of television's ubiquity. It brought its first war, Vietnam, into the living room from ten thousand miles away; it showed us racial explosion across urban America; it covered the campus meetings that revealed the widest generation gap in American history; and it captured, in endless replays, the assassination of three of the country's most popular political leaders. And viewers were also voters. The decade of turbulence scrambled old allegiances and rendered old labels meaningless.

The year 1968 was a tide without a turning. Nixon's election ushered in a new era dominated by the paid commercial and an overall media strategy. Already what the press would call "image makers" or "media mavens" were on their way to becoming at least as important as campaign managers. Charles Guggenheim's twenty-five-minute TV film "A Man From New York," broadcast in the 1964 senatorial contest, purported to show that Robert Kennedy was not really from Massachusetts; four years later Guggenheim portrayed George McGovern as a bombardier in World War II to dispel the notion that he was a craven pacifist. More daringly, political manager David Garth ran John Lindsay for reelection in New York City with commercials in which the mayor admitted to endless small mistakes in office, the better to magnify presumed larger accomplishments.

Guggenheim and Garth were pioneers: the full media impact lay in the seventies, when it replaced more conventional activities. Its muscle was most obvious in determining the schedule of the candidate. Traditionally, managers had tried to get their stalwart in front of as many groups as possible. A heavy speaking schedule gave the candidate a chance to make his views known to a disparate electorate, and if the newspapers covered the meetings, so much the better.

Now, every effort focused on television. Instead of sessions with political groups, the object was a contrived "event." The candidate showed up at a senior citizens' center and delivered a brief statement drawn from some position paper. Television news deadlines determined the timing; the campaign coverage of the previous week determined the issue. As election day approached, two or three of what Daniel Boorstin has called "pseudo events" highlighted the day's schedule. Nothing important was said, but the ninety-second exposure brought the candidate to the voter without the intercession of a party of political organization and showed him concerned about something that pollsters had discovered was on the public mind.

This direct appeal made parties increasingly superfluous. To be sure, they still had the critical line on the ballot; they still had enough registered members to make an endorsement worthwhile. But they were no longer the candidates' principal sponsor. Indeed, they could seldom guarantee a crowd. When that was needed, a few media celebrities could draw a larger audience than a politician's speech.

The parties also lost their traditional recruiting function. Formerly, the ambitious sought political office after a period of party service, often at lowly stations. Now the young headed directly toward electoral office with party registration their only evidence of loyalty. In fact, many considered a close affiliation with day-to-day party affairs to be the mark of a hack; a fresh, nonpartisan face appealed more to the electorate than a veteran party standard-bearer. The spread of primaries at the expense of conventions opened the way to further end runs around the organization. In addition, state after state adopted laws designed to loosen the monopoly of parties over the nominating process, thus magnifying the importance of independents. In some states, for example, an eligible voter need only appear at the polls and declare himself at that moment either a Democrat or a Republican to be entitled to cast a ballot in a party primary.

Initially, reformers rejoiced at these trends, and the regular parties seemed to be the first casualties. But media politics knew no factional boundaries. Just as surely as it undermined traditional party practices, it also withered the voluntary base of reform politics. The parties depended on patronage, reformers on participation. What regulars would do as part of the job, independents would do from commitment. Yet a media campaign did not leave much for volunteers to do.

The new media managers cared little for traditional canvassing where part workers or volunteers went door to door to discover preferences, deliver literature, and argue the candidate's case. The foot soldiers were untrained in modern interviewing techniques; they worked at odd hours; they often returned with useless material; and even good campaigns could not provide full voter coverage. Large banks of telephones were more reliable. Paid operators called scientifically selected numbers; the message was uniform; computers swallowed the responses and spit out the printouts. Ironically, phone banks had originally been a volunteer activity. Supporters took home lists and made personal calls; but better management dictated closer control. The new system is expensive, and there is no way of knowing if phone canvassing, even confine to "prime" lists, is effective; but every campaign for high office finds it necessary.

Polling, too, is an indispensable part of the media campaign. The is not new, but its intensity is. "The calls go out every night randomly, 150 or more," wrote B. Brummond Ayres, Jr., in *The New York Times,* in 1981, of the Reagan Presidency, "to homes across the country." The interviews last a half hour; they ask every kind of question bordering on the voter's interest and public matters. Then the computers whiz and calculators click; "earlier interviews are thrown into the mix" and "in a matter of hours President Reagan and the officials of the Republican National Committee have in hand the latest intelligence needed to tailor a speech, a program or a policy." Richard Werthlin's Washington firm is paid $900,000 a year for this "tracking" of the popular mood.

Previous Presidents relied on a handful of trusted advisers and erratic, and usually unsolicited, reports of party leaders and friends from across the country. But now all campaigns use polls. Indeed, despite their frequent and sometimes flagrant errors, the press and the media treat their results as news stories; columnists scatter ratings throughout their interpretations; analysts worry that their wide use had become a surrogate election, even affecting the actual outcome. Polls are, however, so much a part of the candidate's strategy that some state legislatures have moved against the release of selected parts and require the publication of the full survey. And one poll alone won't do. Anxious managers and candidates can hardly get enough of them, especially in the climactic weeks of the campaign. What is also important is that the survey is bought and requires no use of volunteers.

The media campaign is all business. There is none of the congenial chaos that characterized traditional politics. At headquarters a few people mill about numberless machines. Everything is computerized. Paid employees run the terminals; paid telephoners call numbers from purchased printouts; rented machines slap labels on direct-mail envelopes. Mercenaries grind out "position papers," and press releases are quickly dispatched to a computerized "key" list of newspapers, radio, television stations, columnists, and commentators. "What they have created," wrote the *New York Times* reporter Steven V. Roberts, "is an electronic party."

At the center of the effort is the purchasing of paid television commercials. They are the modern substitute for conventional campaigning. The candidate is not seen live; the message, in fact, is often delivered by a professional voice. The purpose is to project a candidate who is like the viewer, but better: one who arouses but does not agitate; one who elevates but does not disturb; one who exudes morality but not righteousness; one who conveys strength but not arrogance; one who has convictions but avoids controversy. Since such people are in as short supply in private life as in public affairs, a good deal of contrivance is demanded, and the commercial permits it.

The commercial does not seek truth but plausibility. It confines itself to a handful of "issues" that are the candidate's long suit and that are reiterated until the viewer is convinced that these are of paramount interest to other voters even if they are not so to him. The idea is to define the argument on the candidate's own terms. All this is done in the context of constant polling, telephone feedback, and, it must be added, old-fashioned political instinct. As the campaign continues, one spot will be dropped, others altered, and still others emphasized.

The central fact about commercials is their cost. For maximum advantage they are artfully spiced into programs with large voting audiences. Since most advertisers head for the same viewers, the price is very high. In 1980 thirty seconds of the prime-time New York market cost $5,000; ninety seconds cost $15,000. Even in South Dakota these figures ran as high as $250 and $500.

The financial risks attendant on a media campaign are borne solely by the candidate, not by the media managers. Bookings for commercial spots have to be made far in advance and the money paid on the barrelhead. In the past, suppliers of campaign materials—printers, hotels, and airlines—were more tolerant. Some creditors had to wait years for their money and then settled on a percentage, often small, of the original bill.

But now media consultants get their money on schedule. The most common plea at a fund raiser as election day approaches is, "If we don't have the money by tomorrow noon, the candidate is off the air." This is shorthand for saying, "Unless you cough up, the election is over."

The media people have so convinced the public and political donors that the commercial *is* the campaign that only the penurious or uncommitted will resist. And the media's demand is insatiable. If the consultant's polls show the candidate is behind, then a large buy is crucial; if ahead, then the turnout is critical. In either case, the cameras roll and the candidate pays.

Worse still, the media's demand hits the candidate when he is most vulnerable. A whole career seems to ride on the outcome. Hence, the resources of the family are called in, friends enlisted, business and professional associates tapped. For a while this personally very wealthy, the cupboard is soon bare. The only recourse is to go to "political givers," old and new. They have the capacity to underwrite the big loans to cover the up-front money. Yet their liability is very small. (State and federal laws restrict total spending and the amount of individual contributions; everything above those limits must be repaid.)

For the donors it is a cheap ante: they are ultimately repaid by the finance committee. After the election a few galas retire the victors' debt. For the losers, debt is a persistent nightmare.

Many people can afford political giving, but few do it. The result is a hectic and not always elevating courtship of a handful of wealthy people by the candidate and his finance committee. Some potential donors have only a dilettante's interest in politics, but most have interests that are more than marginally related to government. They expect what the trade euphemistically calls "access" to the winner.

The influence of money in American politics is, of course, not new. But the media has introduced a level of spending never known before. In the 1960 presidential campaigns about 10 percent of the budget went to television; by 1980 it had reached 80 percent. David Garth, the most successful practitioner of the new politics, succinctly summed up the present reality when he asserted that political effort outside commercials "is a waste of time and money." The result is that the inordinate power of money in American politics is larger now than it was a generation ago.

Nothing, perhaps, better illustrates today's sharp cleavage with past electioneering than Rep. Millicent Fenwick's 1982 campaign for the United States Senate seat from New Jersey. Now in her seventies, Fenwick grew up with the old politics. "I have a total amateur approach," she told *The New York Times,* reflecting her traditional reliance on volunteer activity. But she reluctantly admitted to hiring a television consultant, studying polls, and submitting to the new fund-raising imperative. "I have never used a television person before, and all this professionalism is not happy-making, being packaged by professionals as though you were some new kind of invention like the splash-free valve on a faucet." Yet soon Fenwick commercials began the "thematic" bombardment, polls suggested tactics, and fund raisers started scrambling. Ironically, she was defeated by a wealthy newcomer who had no reservations about television.

Perhaps an even more telling gauge of the transformation of the political process was Theodore White's bewilderment in covering the presidential election of 1980. Since 1960 he had been the country's premier chronicler of the summit contests. Now, baffled by the new system, and nearly certain it signaled democracy's decline, he left the campaign trail and went home to watch it all on television. Always the quintessential insider, he now felt himself irrelevant bric-a-brac from the age of Dwight Eisenhower. He decided, "I could sit at home and learn as much or more about the frame of the campaign as I could on the road." But in fact, Teddy White, without knowing it, was still at the center of things: all the strategy, all the organization, converged on the screen in front of him, coaxing the voters' acquiescence.

And the voters, more and more, choose to stay away. Ronald Reagan's 1980 presidential victory has been called the most decisive since Franklin Roosevelt's in 1932. Yet it drew the smallest voter turnout in modern history. Just over half of the registered voters exercised their franchise that year, and fewer than 20 percent of adults over eighteen years of age gave the new President a "landslide." This decline in registration and voting and the ascendance of the media is no temporal coincidence Increasingly politics has become a spectator sport, with the public watching without participating. The candidate moves in front of the voters on film, while the continued publication of polls keeps him abreast of the latest standings. Election day thus becomes a time for ratification rather than decision. Today many just don't bother. Worst of all, there ar no signs that this trend will not continue. What if, someday, we give an election and no one comes?

The media, of course, is not wholly responsible for this imperilment. The public's disillusionment with politics and politicians is another cause, and it has happened before. The very size of the country and the aftereffects of the sixties' turbulence among the young create an air of alienation, discouragement, and irrelevance. But the media revolution is truly that, and in some form it is here to stay. Yet it is not immune to change. The convention system replaced caucuses a century and a half ago; primaries replaced conventions in most states in this century; and amendments, court decisions, and congressional legislation have immensely widened voter eligibility. The process has adjusted to changing technology in printing and to the democratization on the telephone and radio. There is no reason why the media revolution can not also be made apt to democratic purposes. But that is the task of the generation that is growing up in it, not those who suffered the shock of its introduction and present triumph.

The Hour of
the Founders

Walter Karp

Exactly ten years ago this August, the thirty-seventh President of the United States, facing imminent impeachment, resigned his high office and passed out of our lives. "The system worked," the nation exclaimed, heaving a sigh of relief. What had brought that relief was the happy extinction of the prolonged fear that the "system" might not work at all. But what was it that had inspired such fears? When I asked myself that question recently, I found I could scarcely remember. Although I had followed the Watergate crisis with minute attention, it had grown vague and formless in my mind, like a nightmare recollected in sunshine. it was not until I began working my way through back copies of *The New York Times* that I was able to remember clear why I used to read my morning paper with forebodings for the country's future.

The Watergate crisis had begun in June 1972 as a "third-rate burglary" of the Democratic National Committee headquarters in Washington's Watergate building complex. By late March 1973 the burglary and subsequent efforts to obstruct its investigation had been laid at the door of the White House. By late June, Americans were asking themselves whether their President had or had not ordered the payment of "hush money" to silence a Watergate burglar. Investigated by a special Senate committee headed by Sam Ervin of North Carolina, the scandal continued to deepen and ramify during the summer of 1973. By March 1974 the third-rate burglary of 1972 had grown into an unprecedented constitutional crisis.

By then it was clear beyond doubt that President Richard M. Nixon stood at the center of a junto of henchmen without parallel in our history. One of Nixon's attorneys general, John Mitchell, was indicted for obstructing justice in Washington and for impeding a Securities and Exchange Commission investigation in New York. Another, Richard Kleindienst, had criminally misled the Senate Judiciary Committee in the President's interest. The acting director of the Federal Bureau of Investigation, L. Patrick Gray, had burned incriminating White House documents at the behest of a presidential aide. Bob Haldeman, the President's chief of staff, John Ehrlichman, the President's chief domestic adviser, and Charles Colson, the President's special counsel, all had ben indicted for obstructing justice in the investigation of the Watergate burglary. John Dean, the President's legal counsel and chief accuser, had already pleaded guilty to the same charge. Dwight Chapin, the President's appointments secretary, faced trial for lying to a grand jury about political sabotage carried out during the 1972 elections. Ehrlichman and two other White House aides were under indictment for conspiring to break into a psychiatrist's office and steal confidential information about one of his former patients, Daniel Ellsberg. By March 1974 some twenty-eight presidential aides or election officials had been indicted for crimes carried out in the President's interest. Never before in American history had a President so signally failed to fulfill his constitutional duty to "take care that the laws be faithfully executed."

It also had been clear for many months that the thirty-seventh President of the United States did not feet bound by his constitutional duties. He insisted that the requirements of national security, as he and he alone say fit to define it, released him from the most fundamental legal and constitutional constraints. In the name of "national security," the President had created a secret band of private detectives, paid with private funds, to carry out political espionage at the urging of the White House. In the name of "national security," the President had approved the warrantless wiretapping of news reporters. In the name of "national security," he had approved a secret plan for massive, illegal surveillance of American citizens. He had encouraged his aides' efforts to use the Internal Revenue Service to harass political "enemies"—prominent Americans who endangered "national security"—prominent Americans who endangered" national security" by publicly criticizing the President's Vietnam War policies.

The farmers of the Constitution had provided one and only one remedy for such lawless abuse of power: impeachment in the House of Representatives and trial in the Senate for "high Crimes and Misdemeanors." There was absolutely no alternative. If Congress had not held President Nixon accountable for lawless conduct of his office, then Congress would have condoned a lawless Presidency. If Congress had not struck from the President's hands the despot's cudgel of "national security," then Congress would have condoned a despotic Presidency.

Looking through the back issues of *The New York Times,* I recollected in a flood of ten-year-old memories what it was that had filled me with such foreboding. It was the reluctance of Congress to act. I felt anew my fury when members of Congress pretended that nobody really cared about Watergate except the "media" and the "Nixon-haters." The real folks "back home," they said, cared only about inflation and the gasoline shortage. I remembered the exasperating actions of leading Democrats, such as a certain

Senate leader who went around telling the country that Senate leader who went around telling the country that President Nixon could not be impeached because in America a person was presumed innocent until proven guilty. Surely the senator knew that impeachment was not a verdict of guilt but a formal accusation made in the House leading to trial in the Senate. Why was he muddying the waters, I wondered, if not to protect the President?

It had taken one of the most outrageous episodes in the history of the Presidency to compel Congress to make even a pretense of action.

Back on July 16, 1973, a former White House aide named Alexander Butterfield had told the Ervin committee that President Nixon secretly tape-recorded his most intimate political conversations. On two solemn occasions that spring the President had sworn to the American people that he knew nothing of the Watergate cover-up until his counsel John Dean had told him about it on March 21, 1973. Form that day forward, Nixon had said, "I began intensive new inquiries into this whole matter." Now we learned that the President had kept evidence secret that would exonerate him completely—if he were telling the truth. Worse yet, he wanted it kept secret. Before Butterfield had revealed the existence of the tapes, the President had grandly announced that "executive privilege will not be invoked as to any testimony [by my aides' concerning possible criminal conduct, in the matters under investigation. I want the public to learn the truth about Watergate. . . ." After the existence of the tapes was revealed, however, the President showed the most ferocious resistance to disclosing the "truth about Watergate." He now claimed that executive privilege—hitherto a somewhat shadowy presidential prerogative—gave a President "absolute power" to withhold any taped conversation he chose, even those urgently needed in the on-going criminal investigation then being conducted by a special watergate prosecutor. Nixon even claimed, through is lawyers, that the judicial branch of the federal government was "absolutely without power to reweigh that choice or to make a different resolution of it."

In the U.S. Court of Appeals the special prosecutor, a Harvard Law School professor named Archibald Cox, called the President's claim "intolerable." Millions of Americans found it infuriating. The court found it groundless. On October 12, 1973, it ordered the President to surrender nine taped conversations that Cox had been fighting to obtain for nearly three months.

Determined to evade the court order, the President on October 19 announced that he had devised a "compromise." Instead of handling over the recorded conversations to the court, he would submit only edited summaries. To verify their truthfulness, the President would allow Sen. John Stennis of Mississippi to listen to the tapes. As an independent verifier, the elderly senator was distinguished by his devotion to the President's own overblown conception of a "strong" Presidency. When Nixon had ordered the secret bombing of Cambodia, he had vouch-safed the fact to Senator Stennis, who thought that concealing the President's secret war from his fellow senators was a higher duty than preserving the Senate's constitutional role in the formation of United States foreign policy.

On Saturday afternoon, October 20, I and millions of other Americans sat by our television sets while the special prosecutor explained why he could not accept "what seems to me to be non-compliance with the court's order." Then the President flashed the dagger sheathed within his "compromise." At 8:31 P.M. television viewers across the country learned that he had fired the special prosecutor; that attorney general Elliot Richardson had resigned rather than issue that order to Cox; that the deputy attorney general, William Ruckelshaus, also had refused to do so and had been fired for refusing; that it was a third acting attorney general who had finally issued the order. With trembling voices, television newscasters reported that the President had abolished the office of special prosecutor and that the FBI was standing guard over its files. Never before in our history had a President, setting law at defiance, made out government seem so tawdry and gimcrack. "It's like living in a banana republic," a friend of mine remarked.

Now the question before the country was clear. "Whether ours shall continue to be a government of laws and not of men," the ex-special prosecutor said that evening, "is now for the Congress and ultimately the American people to decide."

Within ten days of the "Saturday night massacre," one million letters and telegrams rained down on Congress, almost every one of them demanding the President's impeachment. But congressional leaders dragged their feet. The House Judiciary Committee would begin an inquiry into *whether* to begin an inquiry into possible grounds for recommending impeachment to the House. With the obvious intent, it seemed to me, of waiting until the impeachment fervor had abated, the Democratic-controlled committee would consider whether to consider making a recommendation about making an accusation.

Republicans hoped to avoid upholding the rule of law by persuading the President to resign. This attempt to supply a lawless remedy for lawless power earned Republicans a memorable rebuke from one of the most venerated members of their party: eighty-one-year-old Sen. George Aiken of Vermont. The demand for Nixon's resignation, he said, "suggests that many prominent Americans, who ought to know better, find the task of holding a President accountable as just too difficult. . . . To ask the President now to resign and thus relieve Congress of its clear congressional duty amounts to a declaration of incompetence of the part of Congress."

The system was manifestly not working. But neither was the President's defense. On national television Nixon bitterly assailed the press for its "outrageous, vicious, distorted" reporting, but the popular outrage convinced him, nonetheless, to surrender the nine tapes to the court. Almost at once the White House tapes began their singular career of encompassing the President's ruin. On October 31, the White House disclosed that two of the taped conversations were missing, including one between the President and his campaign manager, John Mitchell, which had taken place the day after Nixon returned from a Florida vacation and three days after the Watergate break-in. Three weeks later the tapes dealt Nixon a more potent blow. There was an eighteen-and-a-half-minute gap, the White House announced, in a taped conversation between the President and Haldeman, which had also taken place the day after he returned from Florida. The White House suggested first that the President's secretary, Rose Mary Woods, had accidentally erased part of the tape while transcribing it. When the loyal Miss Woods could not demonstrate in court how she could have pressed the "erase" button unwittingly for eighteen straight minutes, the White House attributed the gap to "some sinister force." On January 15, 1974, court-appointed experts provided by at least five manual erasures. Someone in the White House had deliberately destroyed evidence that might have proved that President Nixon knew of the Watergate cover-up from the start.

At this point the Judiciary Committee was in its third month of considering whether to consider. But by now there was scarcely an American who did not think the President guilty, and on February 6, 1974, the House voted 410 to 4 to authorize the Judiciary Committee to begin investigating possible grounds for impeaching the President of the United States. It had taken ten consecutive months of the most damning revelations of criminal misconduct, a titanic outburst of public indignation, and an unbroken record of presidential deceit, defiance, and evasion in order to compel Congress to take its first real step. That long record of immobility and feigned indifference boded ill for the future.

The White knew how to exploit congressional reluctance. One tactic involved a highly technical but momentous question: What constituted an impeachable offense? On February 21 the staff of the Judiciary Committee had issued a report. Led by two distinguished attorneys, John Doar, a fifty-two-year-old Wisconsin Independent, and Albert Jenner, a sixty-seven-year-old Chicago Republican, the staff had taken the broad view of impeachment for which Hamilton and Madison had contended in the *Federalist* papers. Despite the constitutional phrase ''high Crimes and Misdemeanors,'' the staff report had argued that an impeachable offense did not have to be a crime. ''Some of the most grievous offenses against our Constitutional form of government may not entail violations of the criminal law.''

The White House launched a powerful counterattack. At a news conference on February 25, the President contended that only proven criminal misconduct supplied grounds for impeachment. On February 28, the White House drove home his point with a tightly argued legal paper: If a President could be impeached for anything other than a crime of ''a very serious nature,'' it would expose the Presidency to ''political impeachments.''

The argument was plausible. But if Congress accepted it, the Watergate crisis could only end in disaster. Men of great power do not commit crimes. They procure crimes without having to issue incriminating orders. A word to the servile suffices. ''Who will free me from this turbulent priest,'' asked Henry II, and four of his barons bashed in the skull of Thomas à Becket. The ease with which the powerful can arrange ''deniability,'' to use the Watergate catchword, was one reason the criminal standard was so dangerous to liberty. Instead of having to take care that the laws be faithfully executed, a President, under that standard, would only have to take care to insulate himself from the criminal activities of his agents. Moreover, the standard could not reach the most dangerous offenses. There is no crime in the statute books called ''attempted tyranny.''

Yet the White House campaign to narrow the definition of impeachment met with immediate success. In March one of the members of the House of Representatives said that before voting to impeach Nixon, he would ''want to know beyond a reasonable doubt that he was directly involved in the commission of a crime.'' To impeach the President for the grave abuse of his powers, lawmakers said, would be politically impossible. On the

Judiciary Committee itself the senior Republican, Edward Hutchinson of Michigan, disavowed the staff's view of impeachment and adopted the President's. Until the final days of the crisis, the criminal definition of impeachment was to hang over the country's fate like the sword of Damocles.

The criminal standard buttressed the President's larger thesis: In defending himself he was fighting to protect the "Presidency" from sinister forces trying to "weaken" it. On march 12 the President's lawyer, James D. St. Clair, sounded this theme when he declared that he did not represent the President "individually' but rather the "office of the Presidency." There was even a National Citizens Committee for Fairness to the Presidency. It was America's global leadership, Nixon insisted, that made a "strong" Presidency so essential. Regardless of the opinion of some members of the Judiciary Committee, Nixon told a joint session of Congress, he would do nothing that "impairs the ability of the Presidents of the future to make the great decisions that are so essential to this nation and the world."

I used to listen to statements such as these with deep exasperation. Here was a President daring to tell Congress, in effect, that a lawless Presidency was necessary to America's safety, while a congressional attempt to re-assert the rule of law undermined the nation's security.

Fortunately for constitutional government, however, Nixon's conception of a strong Presidency included one prerogative whose exercise was in itself an impeachable offense. Throughout the month of March the President insisted that the need for "confidentiality" allowed him to withhold forty-two tapes that the Judiciary Committee had asked of him. Nixon was claiming the right to limit the consitutional power of Congress to inquire into his impeachment. This was more than Republicans on the committee could afford to tolerate.

"Ambition must be made to counteract ambition," Madison had written in *The Federalist*. On April 11 the Judiciary Committee voted 33 to 3 to subpoena the forty-two tapes, the first subpoena ever issued to a President by a committee of the House. Ambition, at last, was counteracting ambition. This set the stage for one of the most lurid moments in the entire Watergate crisis.

As the deadline for compliance drew near, tension began mounting in the country. Comply or defy? Which would the President do? Open defiance was plainly impeachable. Frank compliance was presumably ruinous. On Monday. April 29, the President went on television to give the American people his answer. Seated in the Oval Office with the American flag behind him, President Nixon calmly announced that he was going to make over to the Judiciary Committee—and the public—"edited transcripts" of the subpoenaed tapes. These transcripts "will tell it all," said the President; there was nothing more that would need to be known for an impeachment inquiry about his conduct. To sharpen the public impression of presidential candor, the transcripts had been distributed among forty-two thick, loose-leaf binders which were stacked in two-foot-high piles by the President's desk. As if to warn the public not to trust what the newspapers would say about the transcripts. Nixon accused the media of concocting the Watergate crisis out of "rumor, gossip, innuendo,'' of creating a ''vague, general impression of massive wrongdoing, implicating everybody, gaining credibility by its endless repetition.''

The next day's *New York Times* pronounced the President's speech ''his most powerful Watergate defense since the scandal broke.'' By May 1 James Reston, the newspaper's most eminent columnist, thought the President had ''probably gained considerable support in the country.'' For a few days it seemed as though the President had pulled off a coup. Republicans on the Judiciary Committee acted accordingly. On the first of May, 16 of the 17 committee Republicans voted against sending the President a note advising him that self-edited transcripts punctured by hundreds upon hundreds of suspicious ''inaudibles'' and ''unintelligibles'' were not in compliance with the committee's subpoena. The President, it was said, had succeeded in making impeachment look ''partisan'' and consequently discreditable.

Not even bowdlerized transcripts, however, could nullify the destructive power of those tapes. They revealed a White House steeped in more sordid conniving than Nixon's worst enemies had imagined. they showed a President advising his aides on how to ''stonewall'' a grand jury without committing perjury: ''You can say, 'I don't remember.' You can say, 'I can't recall. I can't give any answer to that, that I can recall.' '' They showed a President urging his counsel to make a ''complete report'' about Watergate but to ''make it very incomplete.'' They showed a President eager for vengeance against ordinary election opponents. ''I want the most comprehensive notes on all those who tried to do us in. . . . They are asking for it and they are going to get it.'' It showed a President discussing how ''national security grounds'' might be invoked to justify the Ellsberg burglary should the secret ever come out. ''I think we could get by on that,'' replies Nixon's counsel.

On May 7 Pennsylvania's Hugh Scott, Senate Republican Minority Leader, pronounced the revelations in the transcript ''disgusting, shabby, immoral performances.'' Joseph Alsop, who had long been friendly toward the President in his column, compared the atmosphere in the Oval Office to the ''back room of a second-rate advertising agency in a suburb of hell.'' A week after Nixon's seeming coup Republicans were once again vainly urging him to resign. On May 9 the House Judiciary Committee staff began presenting to the members its massive accumulation of Watergate material. Since the presentation was made behind closed doors, a suspenseful lull fell over the Watergate battleground.

Over the next two months it was obvious that the Judiciary Committee was growing increasingly impatient with the President, who continued to insist that, even in an impeachment proceeding, the ''executive must remain the final arbiter of demands on its confidentiality.'' When Nixon refused to comply in any way with a second committee subpoena, the members voted 28 to 10 to warn him that ''your refusals in and of themselves might constitute a ground for impeachment.'' The ''partisanship'' of May 1 had faded by May 30.

Undermining these signs of decisiveness was the continued insistence that only direct presidential involvement in a crime would be regarded as an impeachable offense in the House. Congressmen demanded to see the ''smoking gun.'' They wanted to be shown the ''hand in the cookie jar.'' Alexander Hamilton had called impeachment a ''National Inquest.'' Congress seemed bent on restricting it to the purview of a local courthouse. Nobody spoke of the larger issues. As James Reston noted on May 26, one of the most disturbing aspects of Watergate was the silence of the prominent. Where, Reston asked, were the educators, the business leaders, and the elder statement to delineate and define the great constitutional issues at stake? When the White House began denouncing the Judiciary Committee as a ''lynch mob,'' virtually nobody rose to the committee's defense.

On July 7 the Sunday edition of the *New York Times* made doleful reading. ''The official investigations seem beset by semitropical torpor,'' the newspaper reported in its weekly news summary. White House attacks on the committee, said the *Times,* were proving effective in the country. In March, 60 percent of those polled by Gallup wanted the President tried in the Senate for his misdeeds. By June the figure had failed to 50 percent. The movement for impeachment, said the *Times,* was losing its momentum. Nixon, it seemed, had worn out the public capacity for righteous indignation.

Then, on July 19, John Doer, the Democrats' counsel, did what nobody had done before with the enormous, confusing mass of interconnected misdeeds that we labeled ''Watergate'' for sheer convenience. At a meeting of the Judiciary Committee he compressed the endlessly ramified scandal into a grave and compelling case for impeaching he thirty-seventh President of the United State. He spoke of the President's ''enormous crimes.'' He warned the committee that it dare not look indifferently upon the ''terrible deed of subverting the Constitution.'' He urged the members to consider with favor five broad articles of impeachment, ''charges with a grave historic ring,'' as the *Times* said of them.

In a brief statement, Albert Jenner, the Republicans' counsel, strongly endorsed Doar's recommendations. The Founding Fathers, he reminded committee members, had established a free country and a free Constitution. It was now the committee's momentous duty to determine ''whether that country and that Constitution are to be preserved.''

How I had yearned for those words during the long, arid months of the ''smoking gun'' and the ''hand in the cookie jar.'' Members of the committee must have felt the same way, too, for Jenner's words were to leave a profound mark on their final deliberations. That I did not know yet, but what I did know was heartening. The grave maxims of liberty, once invoked, instantly took the measure of meanness and effrontery. When the President's press spokesman, Ron Zeigler, denounced the committee's proceedings as a ''kangaroo court,'' a wave of disgust coursed through Congress. The hour of the Founders had arrived.

The final deliberations of the House Judiciary Committee began on the evening of July 24, when Chairman Peter Rodino gaveled the committee to order before some forty-five million television viewers. The committee made a curious spectacle: thirty-eight strangers strung out on a two-tiered dais, a huge piece of furniture as unfamiliar as the faces of its occupants.

Chairman Rodino made the first opening remarks. His public career had been long, unblemished, and thoroughly undistinguished. Now the representative from Neward, New Jersey, linked hands with the Founding Fathers of our government. ''For more than two years, there have been serious allegations, by people of good faith and sound intelligence, that the President, Richard M. Nixon, has committed grave and systematic violations of the Constitution.'' The framers of our Constitution, said Rodino, had provided an exact measure of a President's responsibilities. It was by the terms of the President's oath of office, prescribed in the Constitution, that the framers intended to hold Presidents ''accountable and lawful.''

That was to prove the keynote. That evening and over the following days, as each committee member delivered a statement, it became increasingly clear that the broad maxims of constitutional supremacy had taken command of the impeachment inquiry. ''We will by this impeachment proceeding be establishing a standard of conduct for the President of the United States which will for all time be a matter of public record,'' Caldwell Butler, a conservative Virginia Republican, reminded his conservative constituents. ''If we fail to impeach . . . we will have left condoned and unpunished an abuse of power totally without justification.''

There were still White House loyalists of course; men who kept demanding to see a presidential directive ordering a crime and a documenting ''tie-in'' between Nixon and his henchmen. Set against the great principle of constitutional supremacy, however, this common view was now exposed for what it was: reckless trifling with our ancient liberties. Can the United States permit a President ''the escape accountability because he may choose to deal behind closed doors,'' asked James Mann, a South Carolina conservative. ''Can anyone argue,'' asked George Danielson, a California liberal, ''that if a President breaches his oath of office, he should not be removed?'' In a voice of unforgettable power and richness, Barbara Jordan, a black legislator from Texas, sounded the grand theme of the committee with particular depth of feeling. Once, she said, the Constitution had excluded people of her race, but that evil had been remedied. ''My faith in the Constitution is whole, it is complete, it is total and I am not going to sit here and be an idle spectator to the diminution, the subversion, the destruction of the Constitution.''

On July 27 the Judiciary Committee voted 27 to 11 (six Republicans joining all twenty-one Democrats) to impeach Richard Nixon on the grounds that he and his agents had ''prevented, obstructed, and impeded the administration of justice'' in ''violation of his constitutional oath faithfully to execute the office of President of the United States and, to the best of his ability, preserve, protect, and defend the Constitution of the United States, and in violation of his constitutional duty to take care that the laws be faithfully executed.''

On July 29 the Judiciary Committee voted 28 to 10 to impeach Richard Nixon for ''violating the constitutional rights of citizens, impairing the due and proper administration of justice and the conduct of lawful inquires, or contravening the laws governing agencies of the executive branch. . . .'' Thus, the illegal wiretaps, the sinister White House spies, the attempted use of the IRS to punish political opponents, the abuse of the CIA, and the break-in at Ellsberg's psychiatrist's office—misconduct hitherto deemed too ''vague'' for impeachment—now became part of a President's impeachable failure to abide by his constitutional oath to carry out his constitutional duty.

Lastly, on July 30 the Judiciary Committee, hoping to protect some future impeachment inquiry from a repetition of Nixon's defiance, voted 21 to 17 to impeach him for refusing to comply with the committee's subpoenas. "This concludes the work of the committee." Rodino announced at eleven o'clock that night. Armed with the wisdom of the Founders and the authority of America's republican principles, the committee had cut through the smoke screens, the lies, and the pettifogging that had muddled the Watergate crisis for so many months. It had subjected an imperious Presidency to the rule of fundamental law. It had demonstrated by resounding majorities that holding a President accountable is neither "liberal" nor "conservative," neither "Democratic" nor "Republican," but something far more basic to the American republic.

For months the forces of evasion had claimed that impeachment would "tear the country apart." But now the country was more united than it had been in years. The impeachment inquiry had sounded the chords of deepest patriotism, and Americans responded, it seemed to me, with quite pride in their country and themselves. On Capitol Hill, congressional leaders reported that Nixon's impeachment would command three hundred votes at a minimum. The Senate began preparing for the President's trial. Then, as countless wits remarked, a funny thing happened on the way to the forum.

Back on July 24, the day the Judiciary Committee began its televised deliberations, the Supreme Court had ordered the President to surrender sixty-four taped conversations subpoenaed by the Watergate prosecutor. At the time I had regarded the decision chiefly as an auspicious omen for the evening's proceedings. Only Richard Nixon knew that the Court had signed his death warrant. On August 5 the President announced that he was making public three tapes that "may further damage my case." In fact they destroyed what little was left of it. Recorded six days after the Watergate break-in, they showed the President discussing detailed preparations for the cover-up with his chief of staff, Bob Haldeman. They showed the President and his henchman discussing how to use the CIA to block the FBI, which was coming dangerously close to the White House. "You call them in," says the President. "Good deal," says his aide. In short, the three tapes proved that the President had told nothing but lies about Watergate for twenty-six months. Every one of Nixon's ten Judiciary Committee defenders now announced that he favored Nixon's impeachment.

The President still had one last evasion: on the evening of August 8 he appeared on television to make his last important announcement. "I no longer have a strong enough political base in Congress," said Nixon, doing his best to imply that the resolution of a great constitutional crisis was mere maneuvering for political advantage. "Therefore, I shall resign the Presidency effective at noon tomorrow." He admitted to no wrongdoing. If he had made mistakes of judgement, "they were made in what I believed at the time to be in the best interests of the nation."

On the morning of August 9 the first President ever to resign from office boarded Air Force One and left town. The "system" had worked. But in the watches of the night, who has not asked himself now and them: How would it all have turned out had there been no white House tapes?

America as a Gun Culture

Richard Hofstadter

Senator Joseph Tydings of Maryland, appealing in the summer of 1968 for an effective gun-control law, lamented: "It is just tragic that in all of Western civilization the United States is the one country with an insane gun policy." In one respect this was an understatement: Western or otherwise, the United States is the one country with an insane gun policy." In one respect this was an understatement: Western or otherwise, the United States is the only modern industrial urban nation that persists in maintaining a gun culture. It is the only industrial nation in which the possession of rifles, shotguns, and handguns is lawfully prevalent among large numbers of its population. it is the only such nation that has been impelled in recent years to agonize at length about its own disposition toward violence and to set up a commission to examine it, the only nation so attached to the supposed "right" to bear arms that its laws abet assassins, professional criminals, berserk murderers, and political terrorists at the expense of the orderly population—and yet it remains, and is apparently determined to remain, the most passive of all the major countries in the matter of gun control. Many otherwise intelligent Americans cling with pathetic stubbornness to the notion that the people's right to bear arms is the greatest protection of their individual rights and a firm safeguard of democracy—without being in the slightest perturbed by the fact that no other democracy in the world observes any such "right" and that in some democracies in which citizens' rights are rather better protected than in ours, such as England and the Scandinavian countries, our arms control policies would be considered laughable.

Laughable, however, they are not, when one begins to contemplate the costs. Since strict gun controls clearly could not entirely prevent homicides, suicides, armed robberies, or gun accidents, there is no simple way of estimating the direct political costs, of having lax gun laws. But a somewhat incomplete total of firearms fatalities in the United States as of 1964 shows that in the twentieth century alone we have suffered more than 740,000 deaths from firearms, embracing over 265,000 homicides, over 330,000 suicides, and over 139,000 gun accidents. This figure is considerably higher than all the battle deaths (that is, deaths sustained under arms but excluding those from disease) suffered by American forces in all the wars in our history. It can, of course, be argued that such fatalities have been brought about less by the prevalence of guns than by some intangible factor, such as the wildness are carelessness of the American national temperament, or by particular social problems, such as the intensity of our ethnic and racial mixture. But such arguments cut both ways, since it can be held that a nation with such a temperament or such social problems needs stricter, not looser, gun controls.

One can only make a rough guess at the price Americans pay for their inability to arrive at satisfactory controls for guns. But it can be suggested in this way: there are several American cities that annually have more gun murders than all of England and Wales. In Britain, where no one may carry a firearm at night, where anyone who wants a long gun for hunting must get a certificate from the local police chief before he can buy it, and when gun dealers must verify a buyer's certificate, register all transactions in guns and ammunition, and take the serial number of each weapon and report it to the police, there are annually about .05 gun homicides per 100,000 population. In the United States there are 2.7. What this means in actual casualties may be suggested by the figures for 1963, when there were 5,126 gun murders in the United States, twenty-four in England and Wales, and three in Scotland. This country shows up about as badly in comparative gun accidents and, to a lesser degree, in suicides. There is not a single major country in the world that approaches our record in this respect.

Americans nowadays complain bitterly about the rising rate of violent crime. The gun is, of course, a major accessory of serious premeditated crime. Appealing for stronger gun controls in 1968. President Johnson pointed out that in the previous year there had been committed, with the use of guns, 7,700 murders, 55,000 aggravated assaults, and more than 71,000 robberies. Plainly, stronger gun controls could not end crime, but they would greatly enhance enforcement of the law (as New York's Sullivan Law does) and would reduce fatalities. Out of every one hundred assaults with guns, twenty-one led to death, as compared with only three out of every one hundred assaults committed by other means. In five states with relatively strong gun laws the total homicide rate per 100,000 population—that is, homicides from all causes—runs between 2.4 and 4.8. In the five states with the weakest gun laws this rate varies from 6.1 to 10.6.

In 1968, after the assassinations of Robert F. Kennedy and Martin Luther King, Jr., there was an almost touching national revulsion against our own gun culture, and for once the protesting correspondence on the subject reaching senators and representatives outweighed letters stirred up by the extraordinarily efficient lobby of the National Rifle Association. And yet all that came out of this moment of acute concern was a feeble measure, immensely disappointing to advocates of serious gun control, restricting the mail-order sales of guns. It seems clear now that the strategic moment for gun controls has passed and that the United States will continue to endure an armed populace, at least until there is a major political disaster involving the use of guns.

Today the *urban* population of the nation is probably more heavily armed than at any time in history, largely because the close of World War II left the participating countries with a huge surplus of militarily obsolescent but still quite usable guns. These could be sold nowhere in the world but in the United States, since no other country large enough and wealthy enough to provide a good market would have them. More weapons became available again in the 1950's, when NATO forces switched to a uniform cartridge and abandoned a stock of outmoded rifles. These again flooded the United States, including about 100,000 Italian Carcanos of the type with which John F. Kennedy was killed. Imported very cheaply, sometimes at less than a dollar apiece, these weapons could be sold at enormous profit but still inexpensively—the one that killed Kennedy cost $12.78.

It has been estimated that between five and seven million foreign weapons were imported into the United States between 1959 and 1963. Between 1965 and 1968 handgun imports rose from 346,000 to 1,155,000. Domestic industries that make cheap handguns are approaching an annual production of 500,000 pistols a year. thus a nation in the midst of a serious political crisis, which has frequently provoked violence, is afloat with weapons—perhaps as many as fifty million of them—in civilian hands. An Opinion Research poll of September, 1968, showed that 34 per cent of a national sample of white families and 24 per cent of blacks admitted to having guns. With groups like the Black Panthers and right-wing cranks like the Minute Men, not to speak of numerous white vigilante groups, well armed for trouble, the United States finds itself in a situation faced by no other Western nation. One must ask: What are the historical forces that have led a supposedly well-governed nation into such a dangerous position?

It is very easy, in interpreting American history, to give the credit and the blame for almost everything to the frontier, and certainly this temptation is particularly strong where guns are concerned. After all, for the first 250 years of their history Americans were an agricultural people with a continuing history of frontier expansion. At the very beginning history of frontier expansion. At the very beginning the wild continent abounded with edible game, and a colonizing people still struggling to control the wilderness and still living very close to the subsistence level found wild game an important supplement to their diet. Moreover, there were no enforceable feudal inhibitions against poaching by the common man, who was free to roam where he could and shoot what he could and who ate better when he shot better. Furthermore, all farmers, but especially farmers in a lightly settled agricultural country, need guns for the control of wild vermin and predators. The wolf, as we still say, has to be kept form the door.

Finally, and no less imperatively, there were the Indians, who were all too often regard by American frontiersmen as another breed of wild animal. The situation of the Indians, constantly under new pressures from white encroachments, naturally commands modern sympathy. But they were in fact, partly from the very desperation of their case, often formidable, especially in the early days when they were an important force in the international rivalries of England, France, and Spain in North America. Like the white man they had guns, and like him they committed massacres. Modern Critics of our culture who, like Susan Sontag, seem to know nothing of American history, who regard the white race as a "cancer" and assert that the United States was "founded on a genocide," may fantasize that the Indians fought according to the rules of the Geneva Convention. But in the tragic conflict of which they were to be the chief victims, they were capable of which they were to be the chief victims, they were capable of striking terrible blows. In King Philip's War (1675–76) they damaged half the towns of New England, destroyed a dozen, and killed an estimated one out of every sixteen males of military age among the settlers. Later the Deerfield and other frontier massacres left powerful scars on the frontier memory, and in the formative days of the colonial period wariness of sudden Indian raids and semi-military preparations to combat them were common on the western borders of settlement. Men and women, young and old, were all safer if they could command a rifle. "A well grown boy," remembered the Reverend Joseph Doddridge of his years on the Virginia frontier, "at the age of twelve or thirteen years, was furnished with a small rifle and shot-pouch. He then became a fort solider, and had his port-hole assigned him. Hunting squirrels, turkeys and raccoons, soon made him expert in the use of his gun."

That familiarity with the rifle, which was so generally inculcated on the frontier, had a good deal to do with such success as Americans had in the battles of the Revolution. The Pennsylvania rifle, developed by German immigrants, was far superior to Brown troops. This blunt musket, an inaccurate weapon at any considerable distance, was used chiefly to gain the effect of mass firepower in open field maneuvers at relatively close range. The long, slender Pennsylvania rifle, which had a bored barrel that gave the bullet a spin, had a flatter and more direct trajectory, and in skilled hands it became a precision instrument. More quickly loaded and effective at a considerable distance, it was singularly well adapted not only to the shooting of squirrels but to the woodsman's shoot-and-hide warfare. It struck such terror into the hearts of British regulars as to cause George Washington to ask that as many of his troops as possible be dressed in the frontiersman's hunting shirt, since the British thought "every such person a complete Marksman." The rifle went a long way to make up for the military inconsistencies and indifferent discipline of American militiamen, and its successes helped to instill in the American militiamen, and its successes helped to instill in the American mind a conviction of the complete superiority of the armed yeoman to the military professionals of Europe.

What began as a necessity of agriculture and the frontier took hold as a sport and as an ingredient in the American imagination. Before the days of spectator sports, when competitive athletics became a basic part of popular culture, hunting and fishing probably were the chief American sports, sometimes wantonly pursued, as in the decimation of the bison. But for millions of American boys, learning to shoot and above all graduating from toy guns and receiving the first real rifle of their own were milestones of life, veritable rites of passage that certified their arrival at manhood. (It is still argued by some defender of our gun culture, and indeed conceded by some of its critics, that the gun cannot and will not be given up because it is a basic symbol of masculinity. But the trouble with all such glib Freudian generalities is that they do not explain cultural variations: they do not tell us why men elsewhere have *not* found the gun essential to their masculinity.)

What was so decisive in the winning of the West and the conquest of the Indian became a standard ingredient in popular entertainment. In the penny-dreadful Western and then in films and on television, the western man, quick on the draw, was soon an acceptable hero of violence. He found his successors in the private eye, the F. B. I. agent, and in the gangster himself, who so often provides a semilegitimate object of hero worship, a man with loyalties, courage, and a code of his own—even in films purporting to show that crime does not pay. All mass cultures have their stereotyped heroes, and none and quite free of violence; but the United States has shown an unusual penchant for the isolated, wholly individualistic detective, sheriff, or villain, and its entertainment portrays the solution of melodramatic conflicts much more commonly than, say, the English, as arising not out of ratiocination or some scheme of moral order but out of ready and ingenious violence. Every Walter Mitty has had his moment when he is Gary Cooper, stalking the streets in *High Noon* with his gun at the ready. D. H. Lawrence may have had something, after all, when he made his characteristically bold, impressionistic, and unflattering judgment that "the essential American soul is hard, isolate, stoic, and a killer." It was the notion cherished also by Hemingway in his long romance with war and hunting and with the other sports that end in death.

However, when the frontier and its ramifications are given their due, they fall short of explaining the persistence of the American gun culture. Why is the gun still so prevalent in a culture in which only about 4 per cent of the country's workers now make their living from farming, a culture that for the last century and a half has had only a tiny fragment of its population actually in contact with a frontier, that, in fact, has not known a true frontier for three generations? Why did the United States alone among industrial societies cling to the idea that a substantially unregulated supply of guns among its city populations is a safe and acceptable thing? This is, after all, not the only nation with a frontier history. Canada and Australia have had theirs, and yet their gun control measures are far more satisfactory than ours. Their own gun homicide rates, as compared with out 2.7, range around .56, and their gun suicide and accident rates are also much lower. Again, Japan, with no frontier but with an ancient tradition of feudal and military violence, has adopted, along with its modernization, such rigorous gun laws that its gun homicide rate at .04 is one of the world's lowest. (The land of hara-kiri also has one of the lowest gun suicide rates—about one fiftieth of ours.) In sum, other societies, in the course of industrial and urban development, have succeeded in modifying their old gun habits, and we have not.

One factor that could not be left out of any adequate explanation of the tenacity of our gun culture is the existence of an early American political creed that has had a surprisingly long life, albeit much of it now is in an underground popular form. It has to do with the anti-militaristic traditions of radical English Whiggery, which were taken over and intensified in colonial America, especially during the generation preceding the American

Revolution, and which became an integral part of the American political tradition. The popular possession of the gun was a central point in a political doctrine that became all but sacrosanct in the Revolution: a doctrine that rested upon faith in the civic virtue and military prowess of the yeoman; belief in the degeneration of England and in the sharp decline of "the liberties of Englishmen" on their original home soil; and a great fear of a standing army as one of the key dangers to this body of ancient liberties. The American answer to civic and military decadence, real or imagined, was the armed yeoman.

By the same reasoning the answer to militarism and standing armies was the militia system. It had long been the contention of those radical Whig writers whose works did so much to set the background of American thought, that liberty and standing armies were incompatible. Caesar and Cromwell were commonly cited as the prime historical examples of the destructive effects of political generals on the liberties of the people. The Americans became confident that their alternative device, an armed people, was the only possible solution to the perennial conflict between militarism and freedom. Their concern over the evils of repeated wars and institutionalized armies was heightened by the eighteenth-century European wars in which they were inevitably involved. Blaming the decay that they imagined to be sweeping over England in good part on the increasing role of the military in the mother country, they found their worst fears confirmed by the quartering of troops before the Revolution. John Adams saw in the Boston Massacre "the strongest proof of the danger of standing armies." The Virginian George Mason, surveying the history of the nations of the world, remarked: "What havoc, desolation and destruction, have been perpetrated by standing armies!" The only remedy, he thought, reverting to one of the genial fictions of this school of thought, was the ancient Saxon militia, "the natural strength and only stable security of a free government." Jefferson reverted to the idea of a popular Saxon militia by providing in his first draft of the Virginia Constitution of 1776 that "no freeman shall ever be debarred the use of arms."

Washington, who had to command militiamen, had no illusions about them. He had seen not a single instance, he once wrote, that would justify "an opinion of Militia or raw Troops being fit for the real business of fighting. I have found them useful as light Parties to skirmish in the woods, but incapable of making or sustaining a serious attack." Despite the poor record of militia troops in the Revolution, as compared with the courage and persistence of Washington's small and fluctuating Continental Army, the myth persisted that the freedom of America had been won by the armed yeoman and the militia system, and the old fear of a standing army was in no way diminished now that it was not to be under the command of an English aristocracy but of native American generals. In the mid-1780's, when the Americans had won their independence and were living under the Articles of Confederation, Secretary of War Henry Knox found himself the administrator of an army of about seven hundred men. In the 1790's, when it was proposed under the Constitution to add only about five hundred more, Pennsylvania Democrat Senator William Maclay anxiously observed that the government seemed to be "laying the foundation of a standing army"! Only the disastrous performance of militiamen in the War of 1812 persuaded many

American leaders that the militia was a slender reed upon which to rest the security of the nation.

In the meantime the passion for a popular militia as against a professional army had found its permanent embodiment in the Second Amendment to the Constitution: "A well regulated Militia, being necessary to the security of a free State, the right of the people to keep and bear Arms, shall not be infringed." By its inclusion in the Bill of Rights, the right to bear arms thus gained permanent sanction in the nation to bear arms thus gained permanent sanction in the nation, but it came to be regarded as an item on the basic list of guarantees of *individual* liberties. Plainly it was not meant as such. The right to bear arms was a *collective,* not an individual, right, closely linked to the civic need (especially keen in the absence of a sufficient national army) for "a well regulated Militia." It was, in effect, a promise that Congress would not be able to bar the states from doing whatever was necessary to maintain well-regulated militias.

The Supreme Court has more than once decided that the Second Amendment does not bar certain state or federal gun controls. In 1886 it upheld an Illinois statute forbidding bodies of men to associate in military organizations or to drill or parade with arms in cities or towns. When Congress passed the National Firearms Act of 1934 forbidding the transportation in interstate commerce of unregistered shotguns, an attempt to invoke the Second Amendment against the law was rejected by the Court in what is now the leading case on the subject, *United States v. Miller* (1939). In this case the Court, ruling on the prosecution of two men who had been convicted of violating the National Firearms Act by taking an unregistered sawed-off shotgun across state lines, concluded that the sawed-off shotgun across state lines, concluded that the sawed-off shotgun had no "reasonable relationship to the prevention, preservation, or efficiency of a well-regulated militia." The Court ruled that since the gun in question was not part of ordinary military equipment, its use was unrelated to the common defense. The Court further found that the clear purpose of the Second Amendment was to implement the constitutional provision for "calling forth the Militia to execute the Laws of the Union, suppress insurrections and repel invasions." and declared that the Second Amendment "must be interpreted and applied with that end in view."

While the notion that "the right to bear arms" is inconsistent with state or federal gun regulation is largely confined to the obstinate lobbyists of the National Rifle Association, another belief of American gun enthusiasts enjoys a very wide currency in the United States, extending to a good many liberals, civil libertarians, and even radicals. It is the idea that popular access to arms is an important counterpoise to tyranny. A historian, recently remonstrating against our gun policies, was asked by a sympathetic liberal listener whether it was not true, for example, that one of the first acts of the Nazis had been to make it impossible for the nonparty, nonmilitary citizen to have a gun—the assumption being that the German people had thus lost their last barrier to tyranny. In fact Nazi gun policies were of no basic consequence: the democratic game had been lost long before, when legitimate authorities under the Weimar Republic would not or could not stop uniformed groups of Nazi terrorists from meetings and when the courts and the Reich Ministry of Justice did not act firmly and consistently to punish the makers of any Nazi *Putsch* according to law. It is not strong and firm governments but weak ones, incapable of exerting their regulatory and punitive powers, that are overthrown by tyrannies. Nonetheless, the American historical mythology about the protective value of guns has survived the modern technologies era in all the glory of its naïveté, and it has been taken over from the whites by some young blacks, notably the Panthers, whose accumulations of arms have thus far proved more lethal to themselves than to anyone else. In all societies the presence of small groups of uncontrolled and unauthorized men in unregulated possession of arms is recognized to be dangerous. A query therefore must ring in our heads: those endangered ask to have such men disarmed, while in the United States along they insist on arming themselves?

A further point is of more than symptomatic interest: the most gun-addicted sections of the United States are the South and the Southwest. In 1968, when the House voted for a mild bill to restrict the mail-order sale of rifles, shotguns, and ammunition, all but a few of the 118 votes against it came from these regions. This no doubt has something to do with the rural character of these regions, but it also stems from another consideration: in the historic system of the South, having a gun was a white prerogative. From the days of colonial slavery, when white indentured servants were permitted, and under some circumstances encouraged, to have guns, blacks, whether slave or free, were denied the right. The gun, though it had a natural place in the South's outdoor culture, as well as a necessary place in the work of slave patrols, was also an important symbol of white male status. Students in the Old South took guns to college as a matter of course. In 1840 an undergraduate at the University of Virginia killed a professor during a night revelry that was frequently punctuated by gunfire. Thomas Hart Benton, later to be a distinguished Missouri senator, became involved, during his freshman year at the University of North Carolina, in a brawl in which he drew a pistol on another student, and was spared serious trouble only when a professor disarmed him. He was sixteen years old at the time. In the light of the long white effort to maintain a gun monopoly, it is hardly surprising, though it may be discouraging, to see militant young blacks borrowing the white man's mystique and accepting the gun as their instrument. "A gun is status— that's why they call it an equalizer," said a young Chicago black a few years ago. "What's happening today is that everybody's getting more and more equal became everybody's got one."

But perhaps more than anything else in the state of American gun controls is evidence of one of the failures of federalism: the purchase and possession of guns in the United States is controlled by a chaotic jumble of twenty thousand state and local laws that collectively are wholly inadequate to the protection of the people and that operate in such a way that areas with poor controls undermine those with better ones. No such chaos would be tolerated, say, in the field of automobile registration. The automobile, like the gun, is a lethal instrument, and the states have recognized it as such by requiring that each driver as well as each car must be registered and that each driver as well as each car must be registered and that each driver must meet certain specified qualifications. It is mildly inconvenient to conform, but no one seriously objects to the general principle, as gun lobbyists do to gun registration. However, as the United States became industrial and urban, the personnel of its national and state legislatures remained to a very considerable degree small town and rural, and under the seniority system that prevails in Congress, key posts on committees have long been staffed by aging members from small-town districts—worse still, from small-town districts in regions where there is little or no party competition and hence little turnover in personnel. Many social reforms have been held back long after their time was ripe by this rural-seniority political culture. Gun control is another such reform: American legislators have been inordinately responsive to the tremendous lobby maintained by the National Rifle Association, in tandem with gunmakers and importers, military sympathizers, and far-right organizations. A nation that could not devise a system of gun control after its experiences of the 1960's and at a moment of profound popular revulsion against guns, is not likely to get such a system in the calculable future. One must wonder how grave a domestic gun catastrophe would have to be in order to persuade us. How far must things go?